A PLUME BOOK

# GRIMMER TALES

**ERIK BERGSTROM** lives and works in New York City as an artist and stand-up comedian. His work has been hung in numerous galleries and thousands of homes. He drinks enough coffee to kill a small horse. He doesn't know why his coffee drinking is killing horses. He really wishes it would stop. Please make it stop. He hopes his drawings of cartoon eggs will make it stop.

# 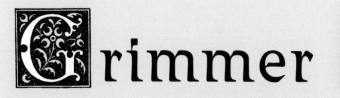rimmer ales

## A Wicked Collection of
## Happily Never After Stories

## Erik Bergstrom

A PLUME BOOK

PLUME
Published by the Penguin Group
Penguin Group (USA) Inc., 375 Hudson Street, New York, New York 10014, U.S.A. • Penguin Group (Canada), 90 Eglinton
Avenue East, Suite 700, Toronto, Ontario, Canada M4P 2Y3 (a division of Pearson Penguin Canada Inc.) • Penguin Books
Ltd., 80 Strand, London WC2R 0RL, England • Penguin Ireland, 25 St. Stephen's Green, Dublin 2, Ireland (a division of
Penguin Books Ltd.) • Penguin Group (Australia), 250 Camberwell Road, Camberwell, Victoria 3124, Australia (a division
of Pearson Australia Group Pty. Ltd.) • Penguin Books India Pvt. Ltd., 11 Community Centre, Panchsheel Park, New Delhi
– 110 017, India • Penguin Group (NZ), 67 Apollo Drive, Rosedale, North Shore 0632, New Zealand (a division of Pearson New
Zealand Ltd.) • Penguin Books (South Africa) (Pty.) Ltd., 24 Sturdee Avenue, Rosebank, Johannesburg 2196, South Africa

Penguin Books Ltd., Registered Offices: 80 Strand, London WC2R 0RL, England
First published by Plume, a member of Penguin Group (USA) Inc.

First Printing, January 2010
10  9  8  7  6  5  4  3  2  1

Copyright © Erik Bergstrom, 2009
All rights reserved

 REGISTERED TRADEMARK—MARCA REGISTRADA

CIP data is available.
ISBN 978-0-452-29602-2

Printed in Mexico
Set in American Typewriter

PUBLISHER'S NOTE
This is a work of fiction. Names, characters, places, and incidents are either the product of the author's imagination or
are used fictitiously, and any resemblance to actual persons, living or dead, business establishments, events, or locales
is entirely coincidental.
The scanning, uploading, and distribution of this book via the Internet or via any other means without the permission of
the publisher is illegal and punishable by law. Please purchase only authorized electronic editions, and do not participate
in or encourage electronic piracy of copyrighted materials. Your support of the author's rights is appreciated.

In memory of my Grandpa Larry,
the best breakfast eater I've ever known.

# ACKNOWLEDGMENTS

A special thanks to Sarah Bowlin, Seth Fishman,
Anna Sternoff, Anna Boman,
and to buckets and buckets of coffee

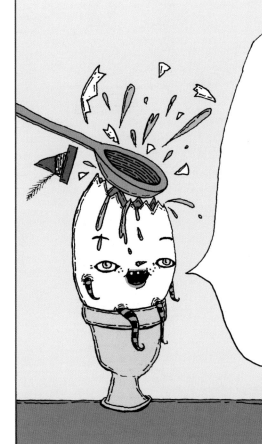

Hey Folks!

Welcome to *Grimmer Tales*, a collection that takes you to a dark and magical place near and dear to my heart. Back in the old (old with an e, actually) days, fairy tales were scary, full of blood and trickery. They taught you something—don't trust strangers, never tell a lie! But nowadays, fairy tales are gentle and fluffy. There's simply no room for screaming or sobbing anymore. And nobody learns anything except that being a spoiled princess will still get you your way. I'd bet the Brothers Grimm are rolling in their graves.

I'll let you in on a secret only my shrink knows: as a kid I wished my bedtime stories were a little more crazy, so when I became an artist I started doodling them—Rapunzel would lose her head when someone tugged on her braid and those snotty brats would get eaten by the witch. Never bothered me (although my shrink has a thing or two to say about it). Personally, I think the world could use a taste of the warped, creepy, and bloody, once in a while. So welcome to *Grimmer Tales*. If nothing else, I hope you'll take away a true fright at that noise under your bed.

Sleep tight!

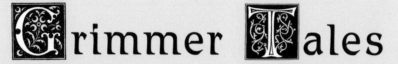

Grimmer Tales

# Little Boy Blew

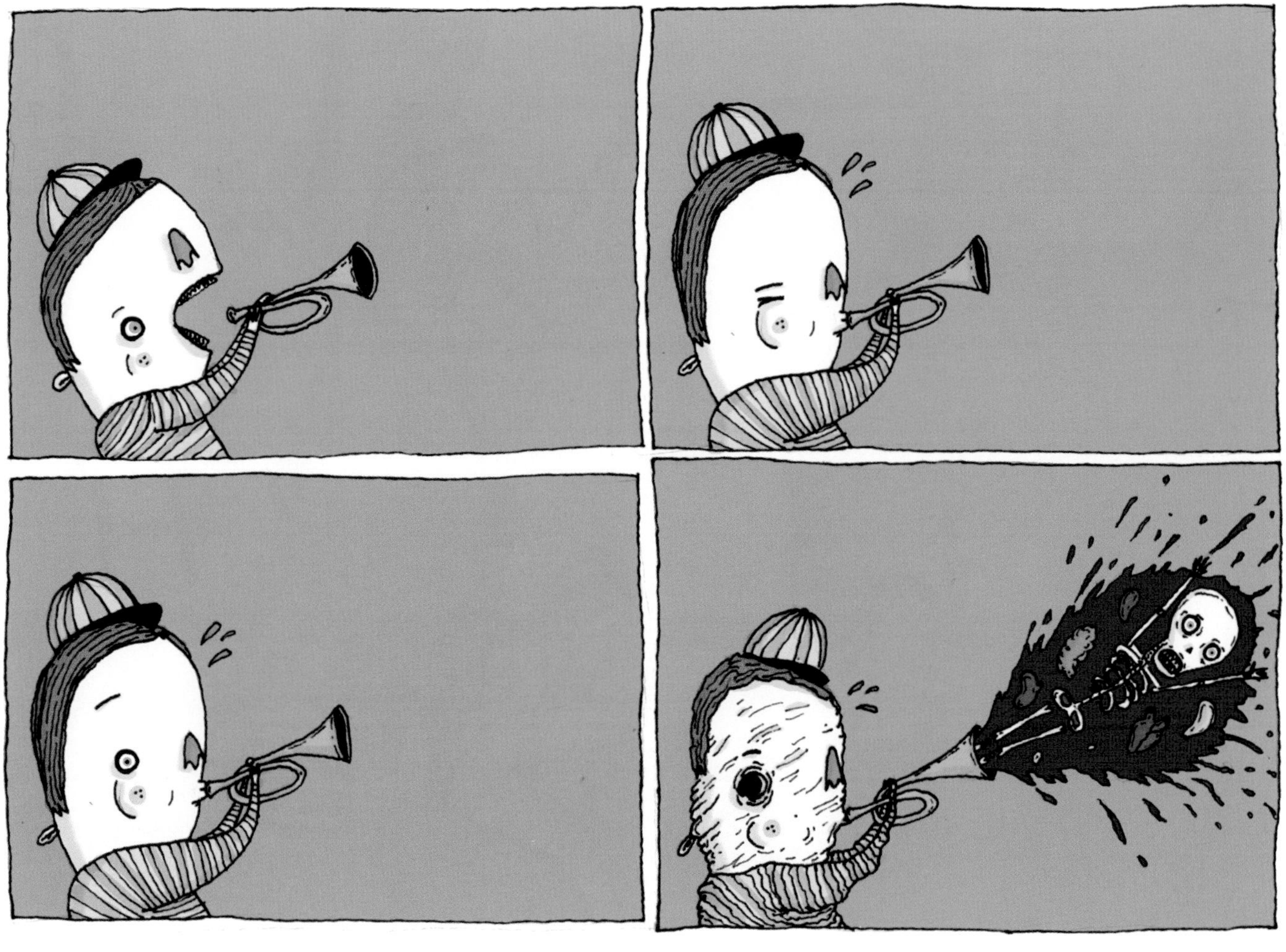

Pinocchio's Wife

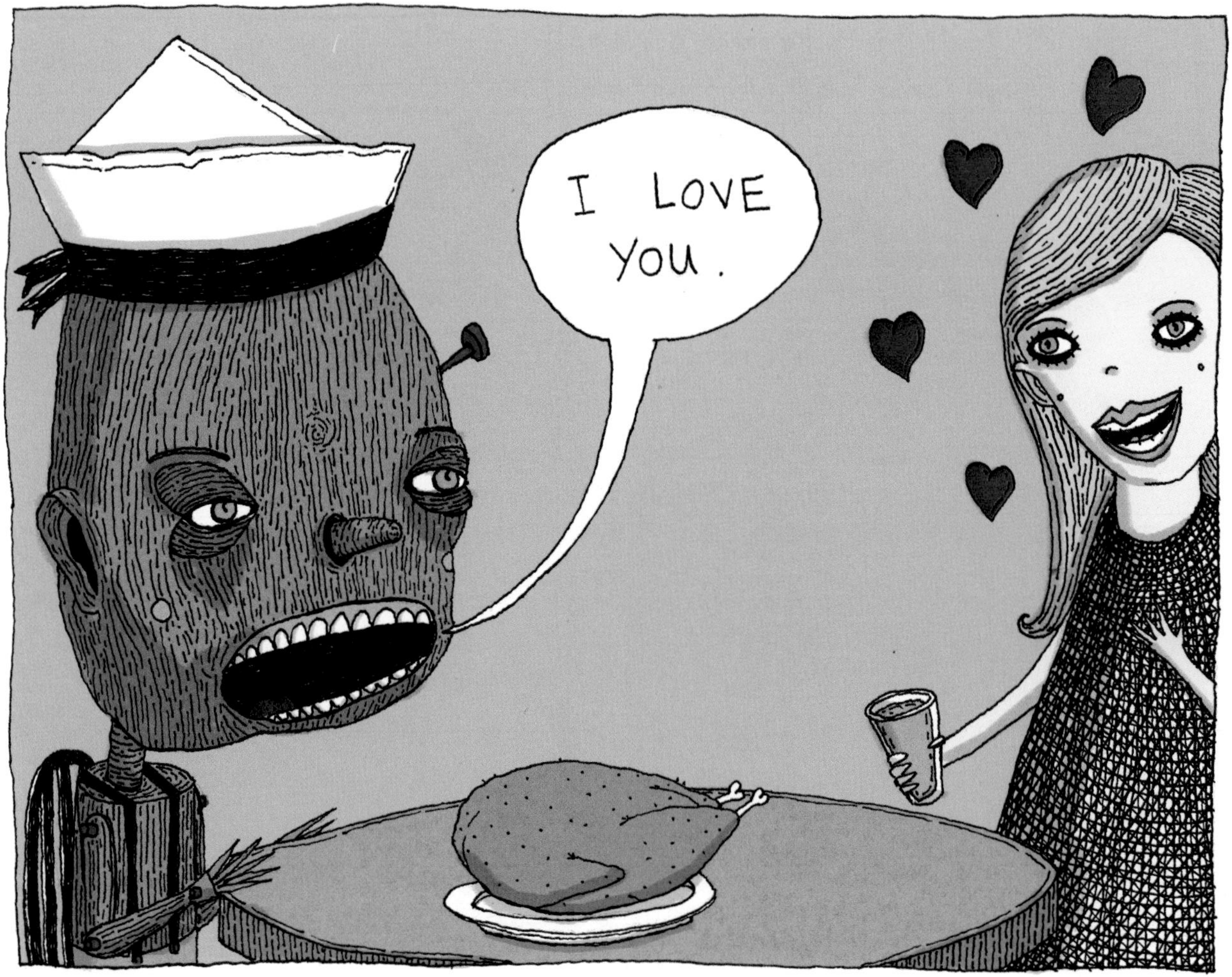
I LOVE YOU.

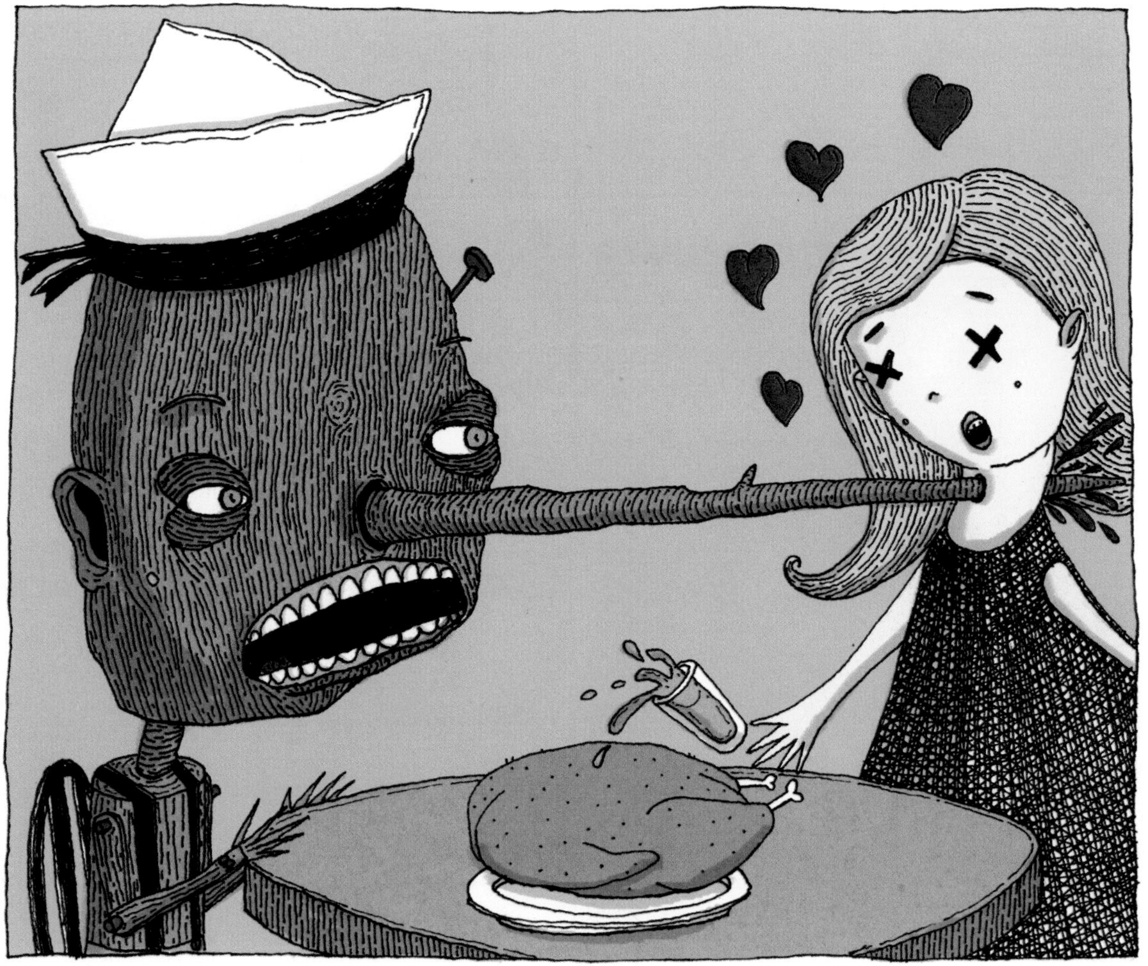

Magic Beans

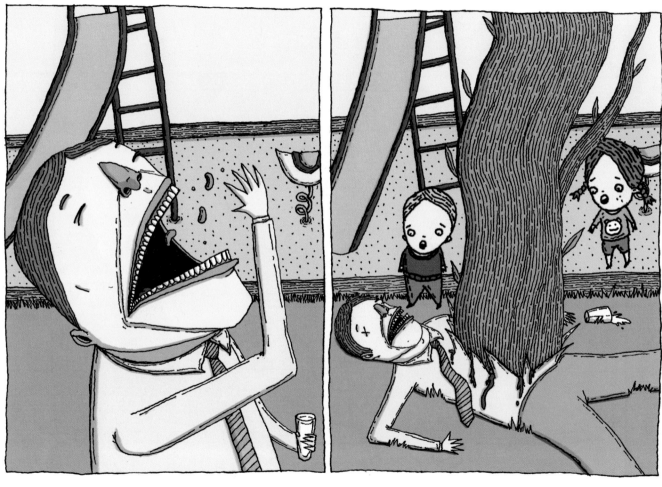

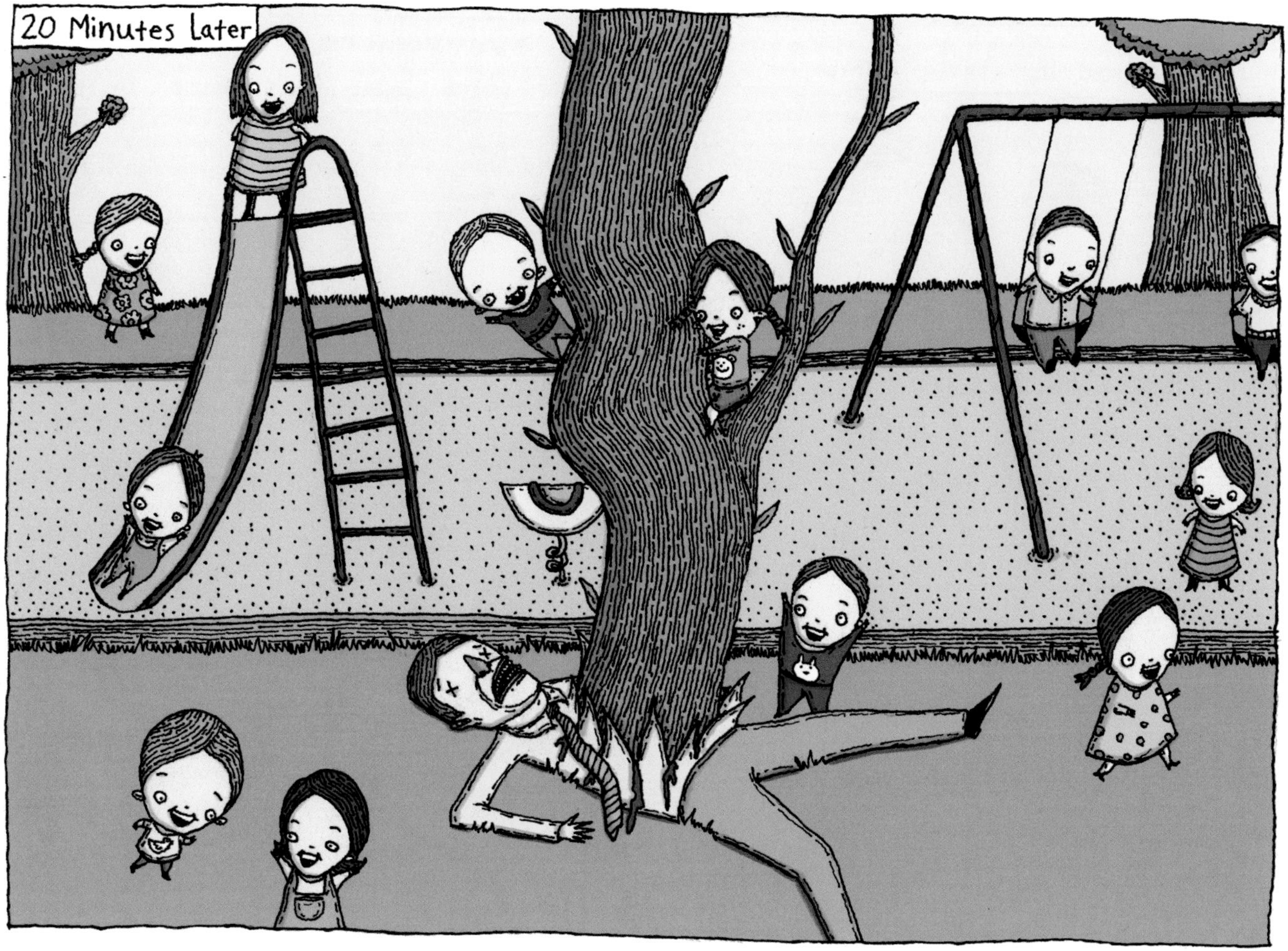
20 Minutes Later

Baaaad Ass

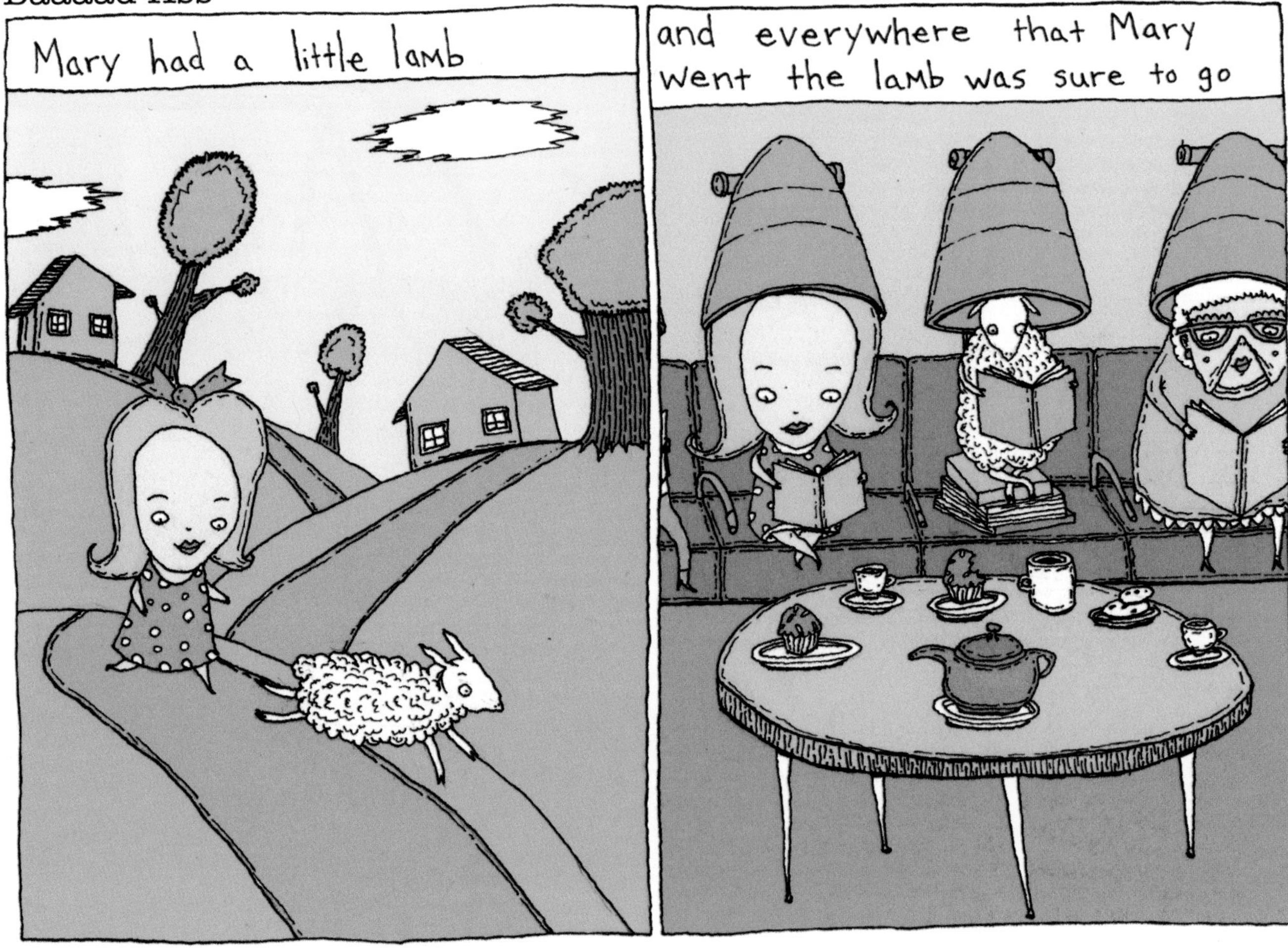
Mary had a little lamb
and everywhere that Mary went the lamb was sure to go

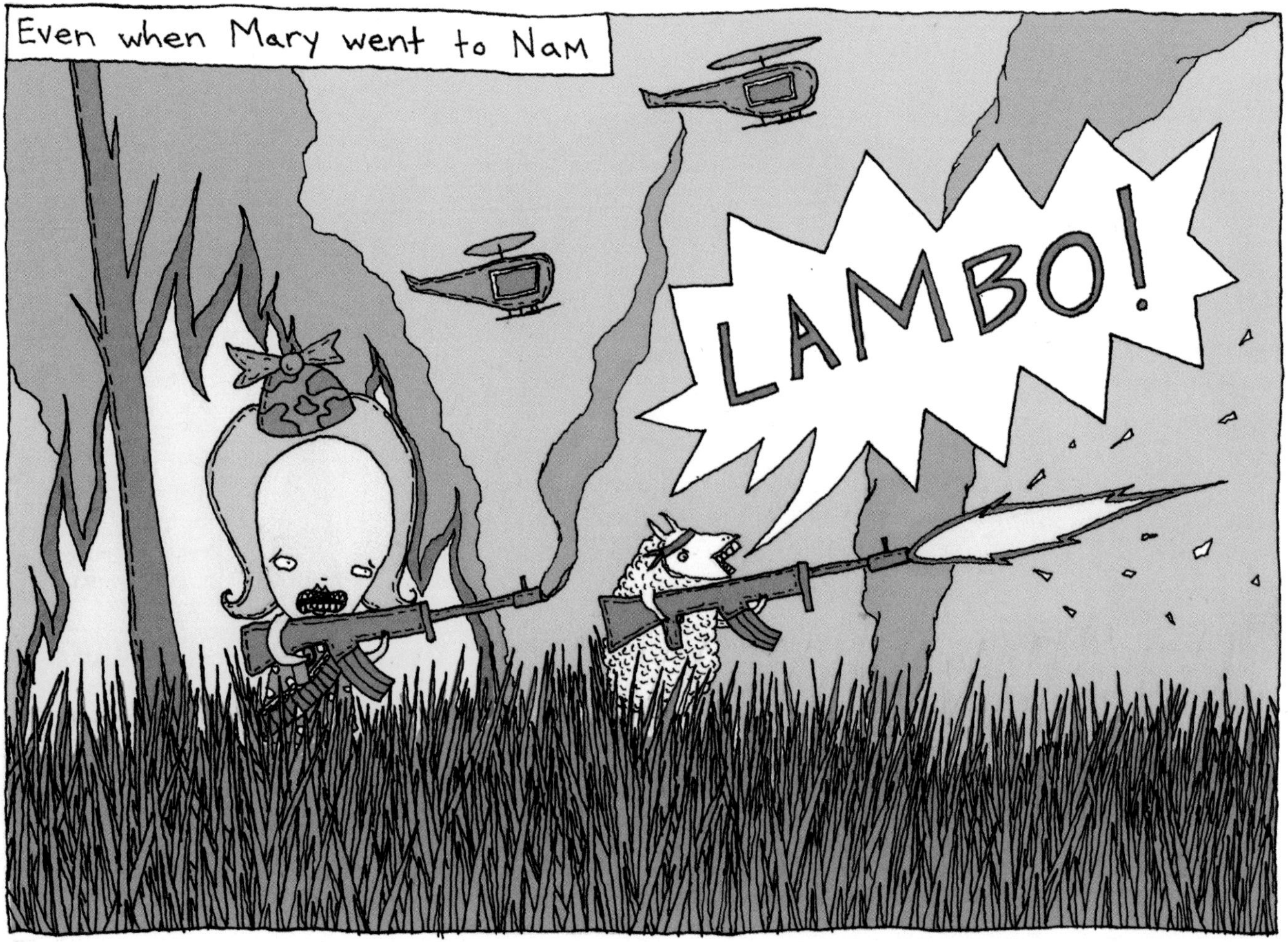
Even when Mary went to NaM
LAMBO!

## Perfect Fit

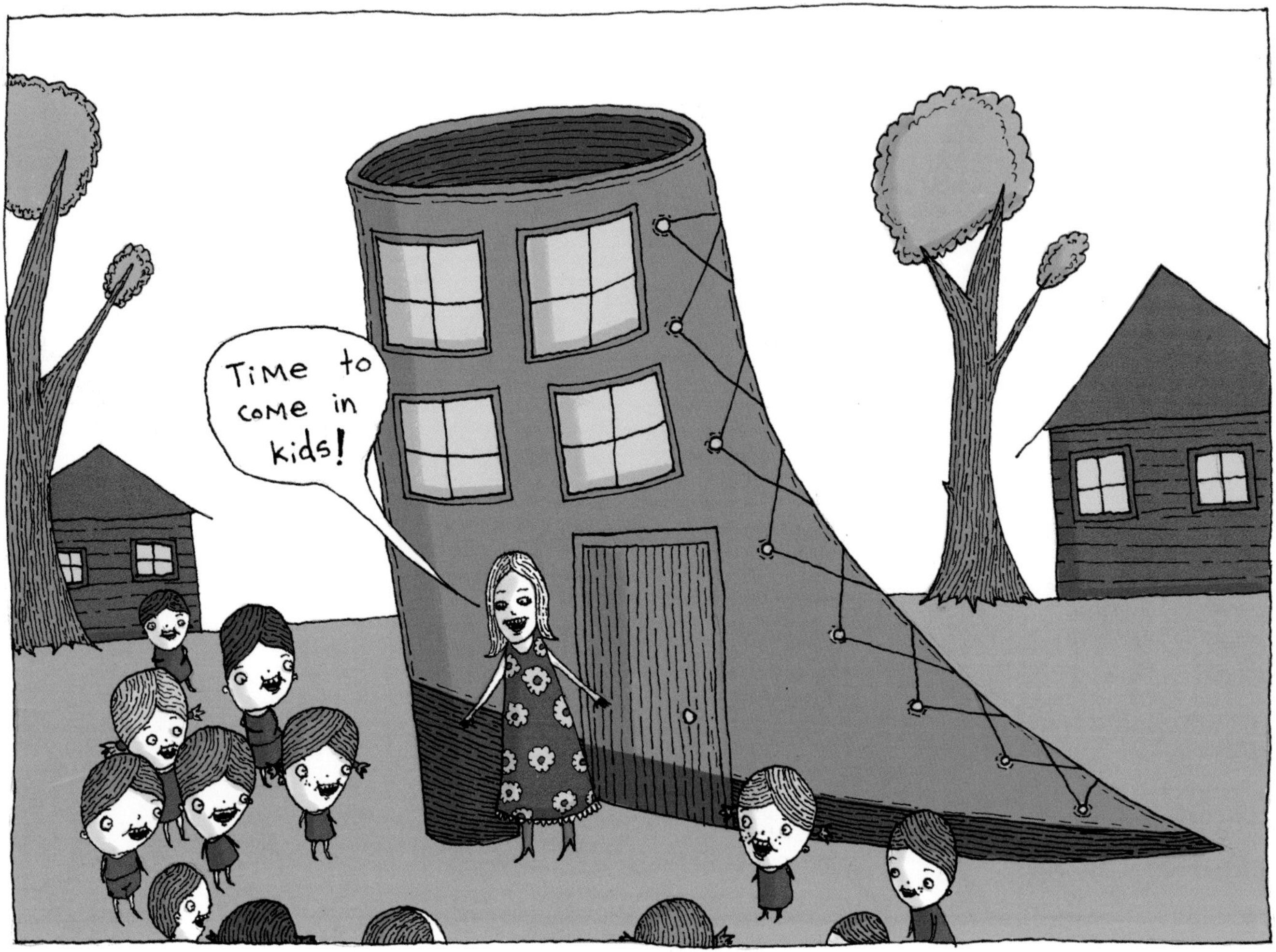
Time to come in kids!

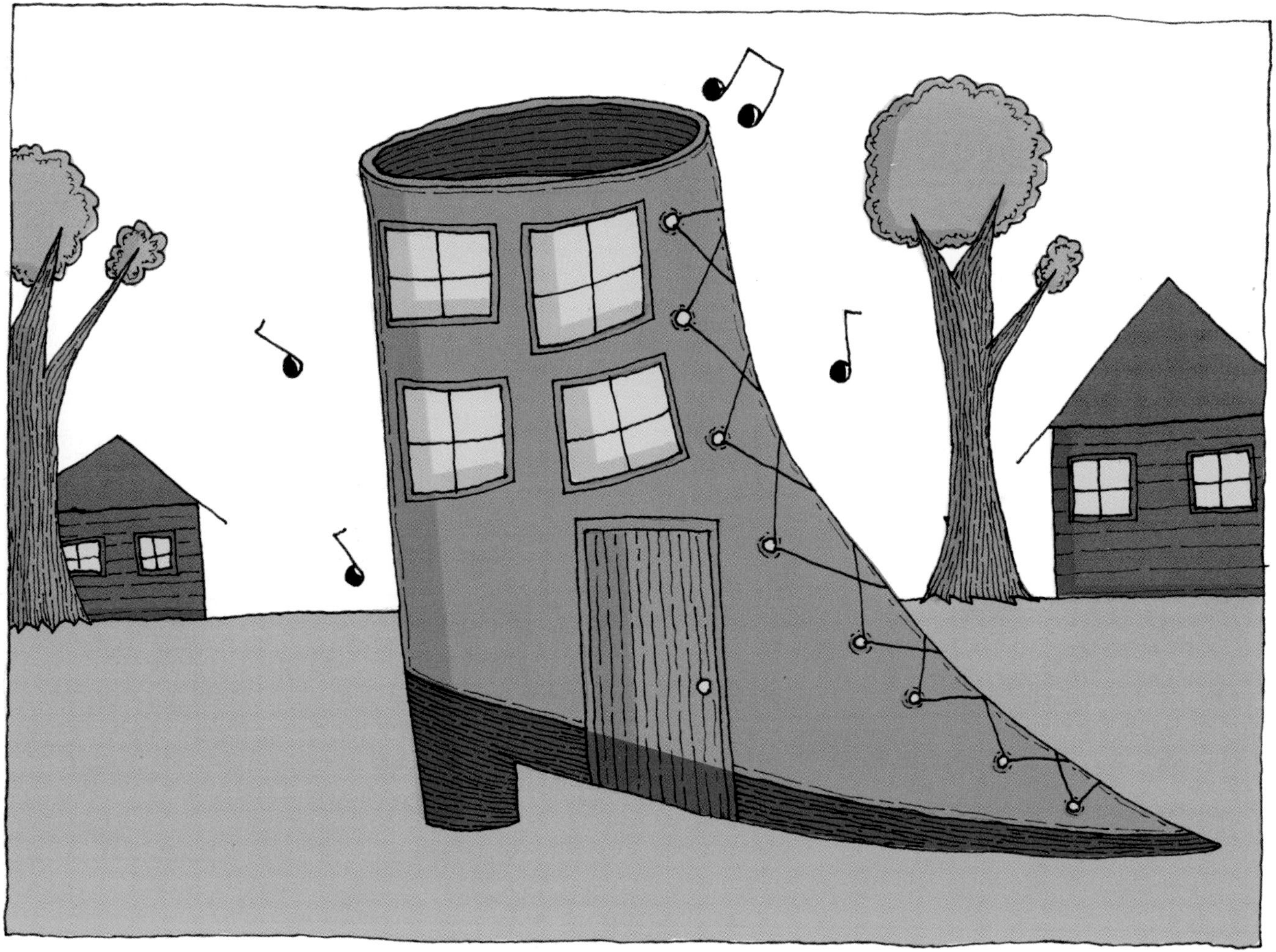

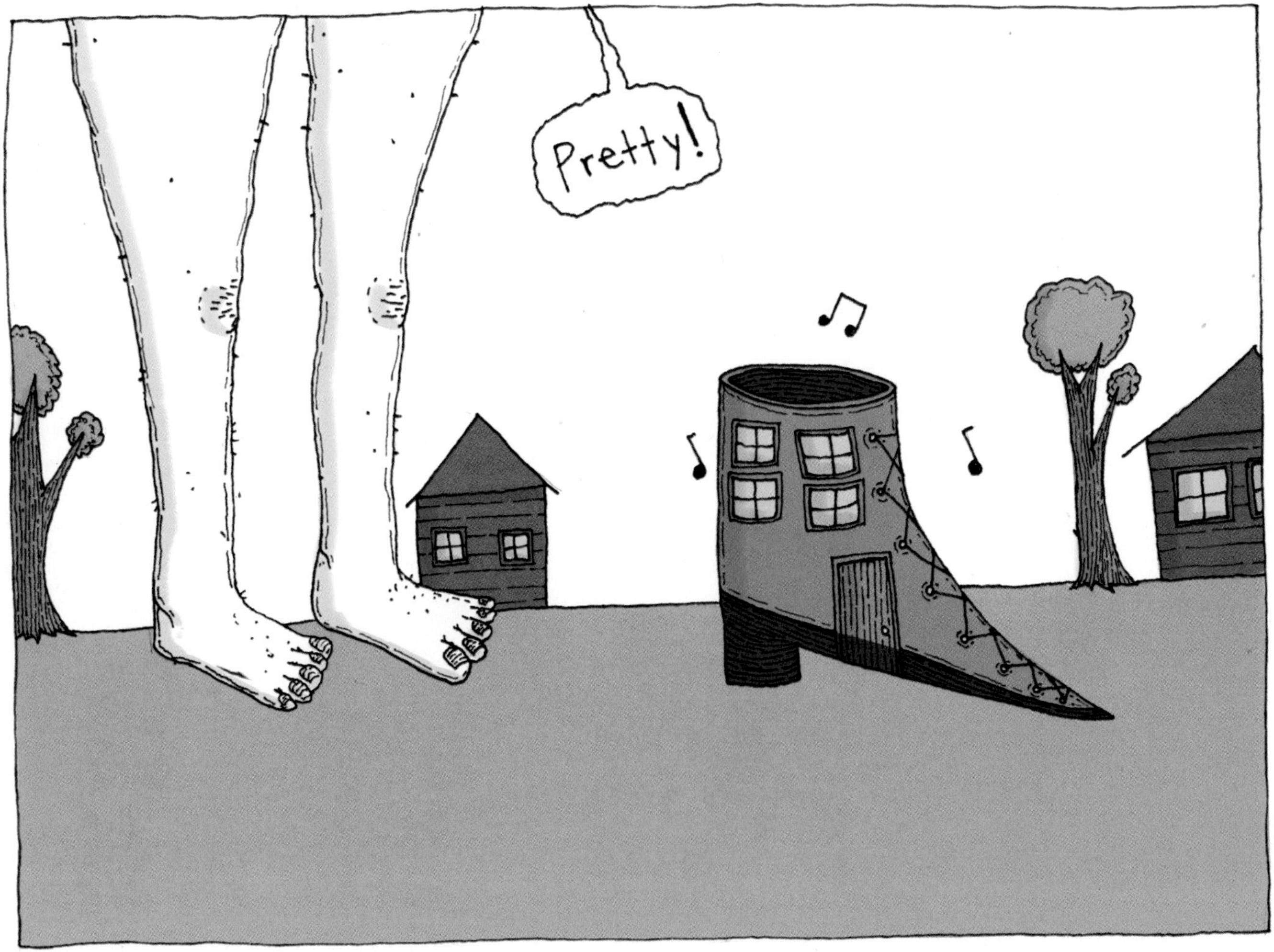
Pretty!

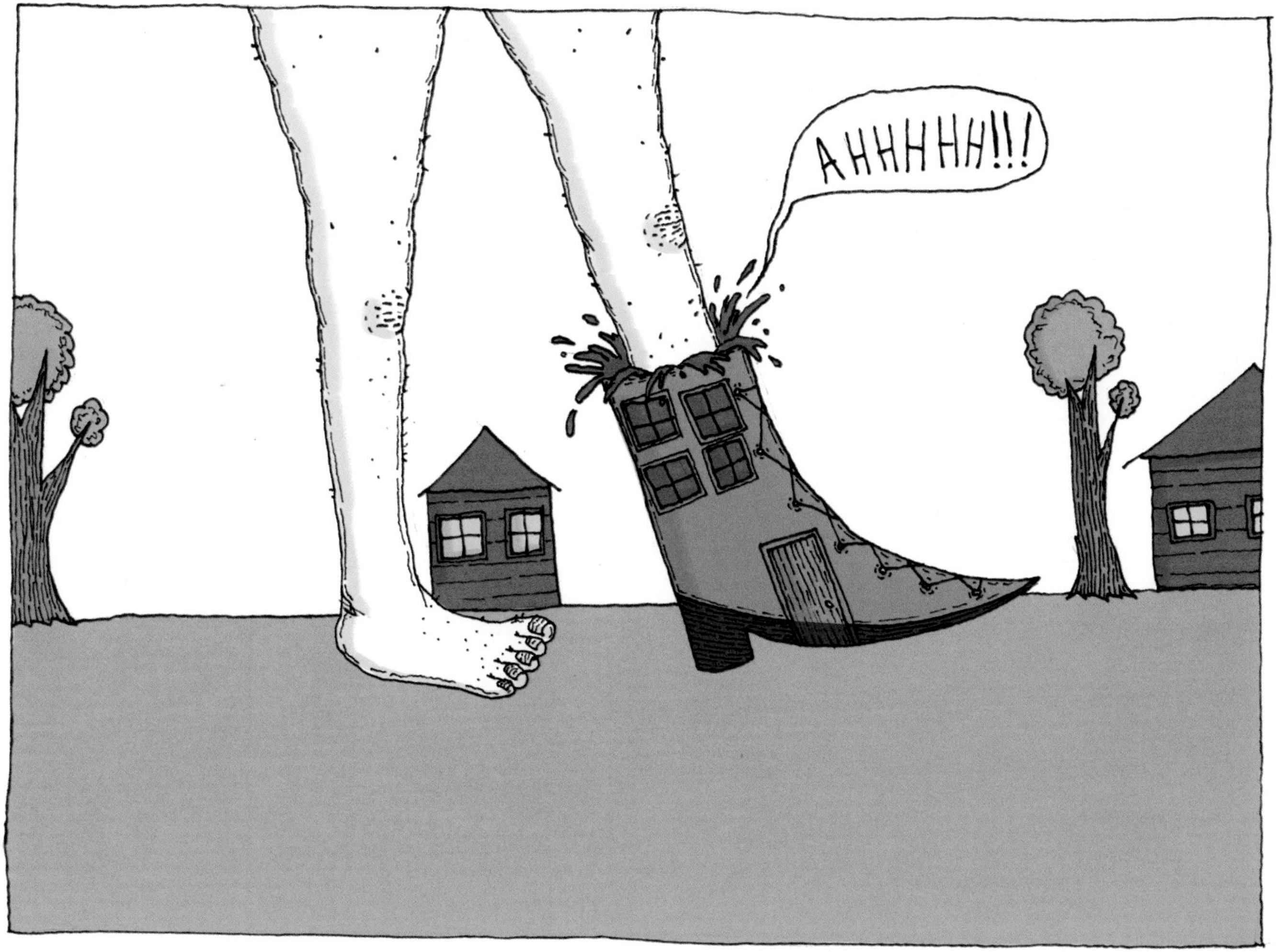
AHHHHH!!!

After Snow White

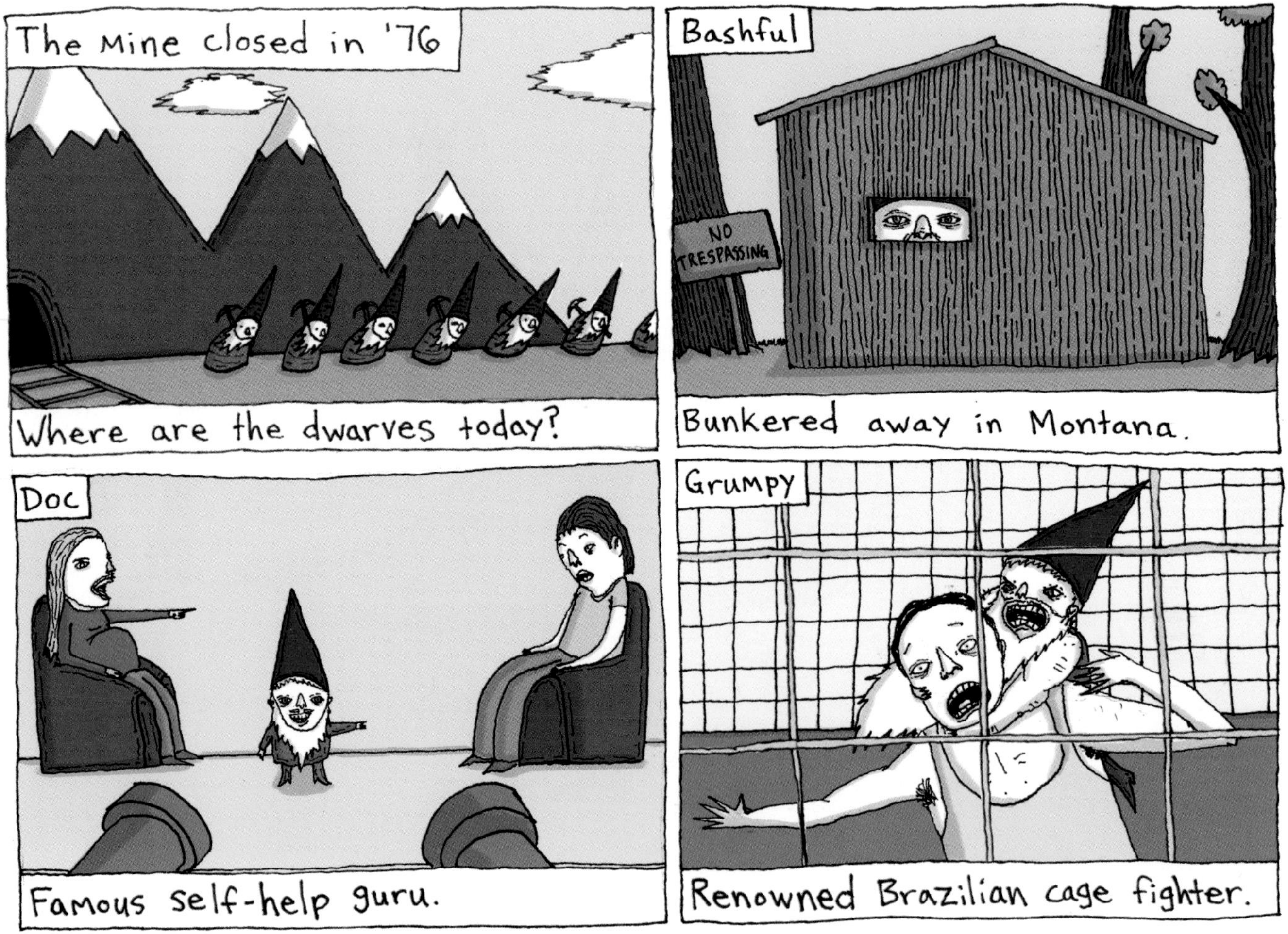
The Mine closed in '76
Where are the dwarves today?
Bashful
NO TRESPASSING
Bunkered away in Montana.
Doc
Famous self-help guru.
Grumpy
Renowned Brazilian cage fighter.

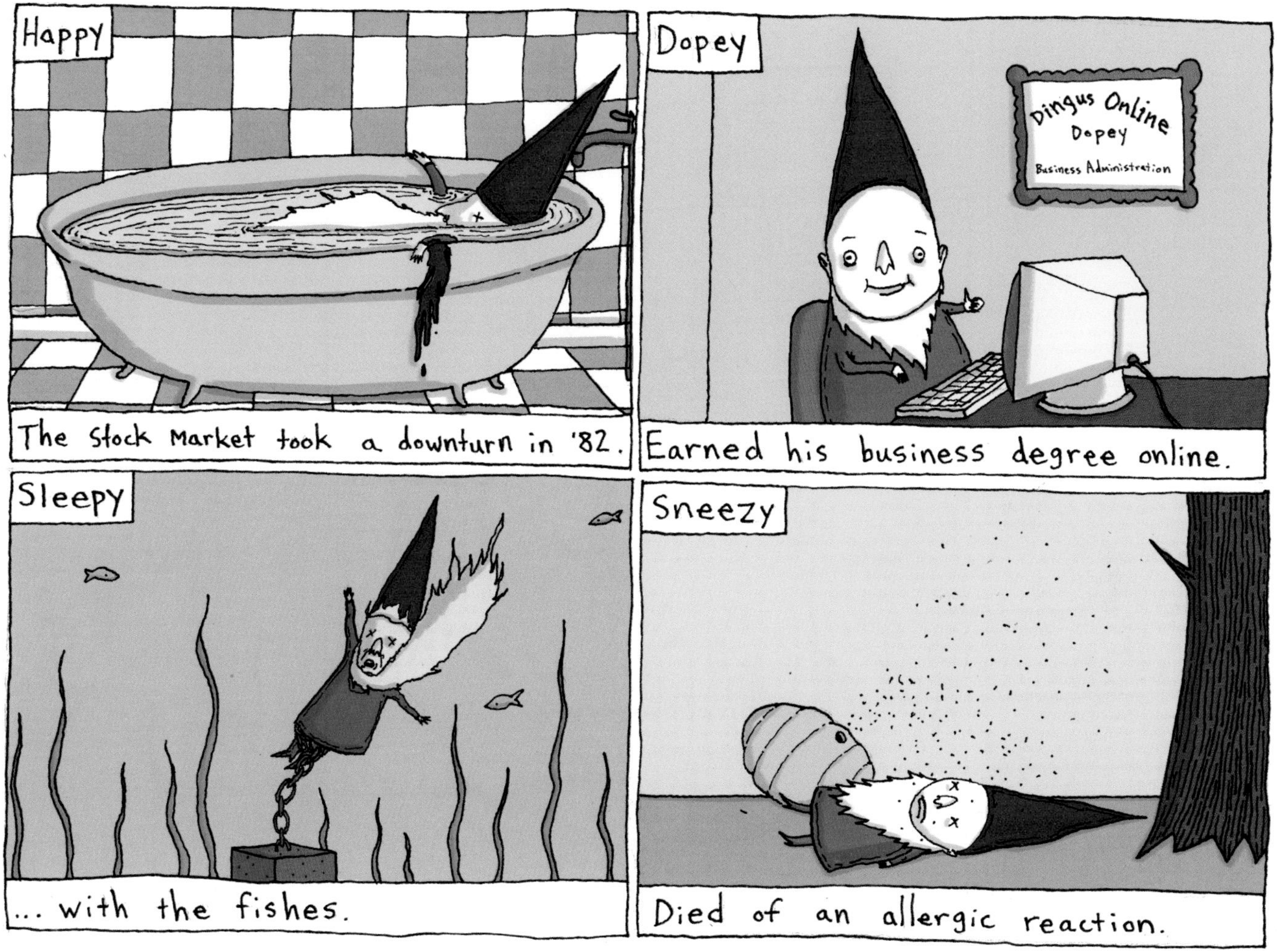
Happy
The Stock Market took a downturn in '82.
Dopey
Dingus Online
Dopey
Business Administration
Earned his business degree online.
Sleepy
... with the fishes.
Sneezy
Died of an allergic reaction.

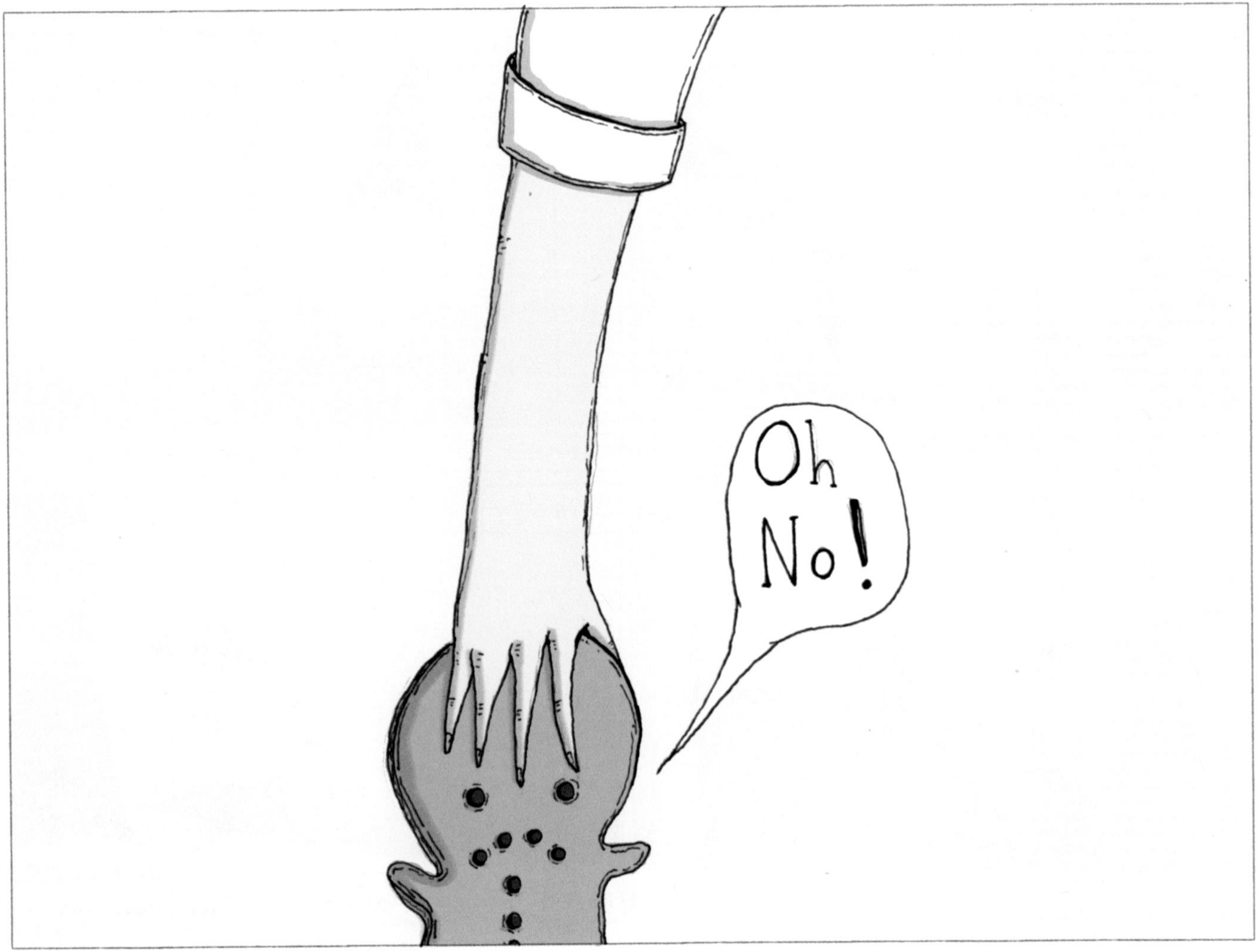
Oh No!

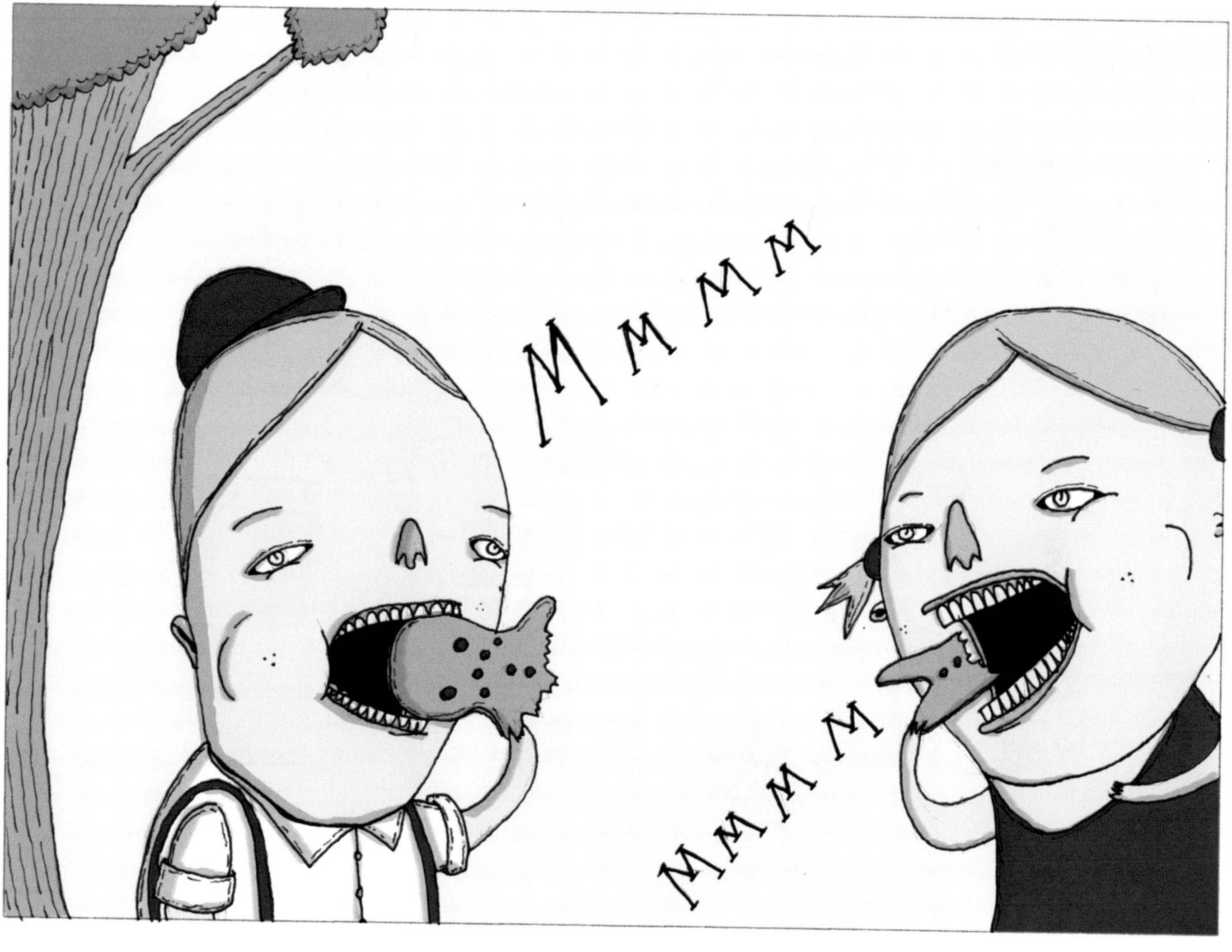

MMMM
MMMM

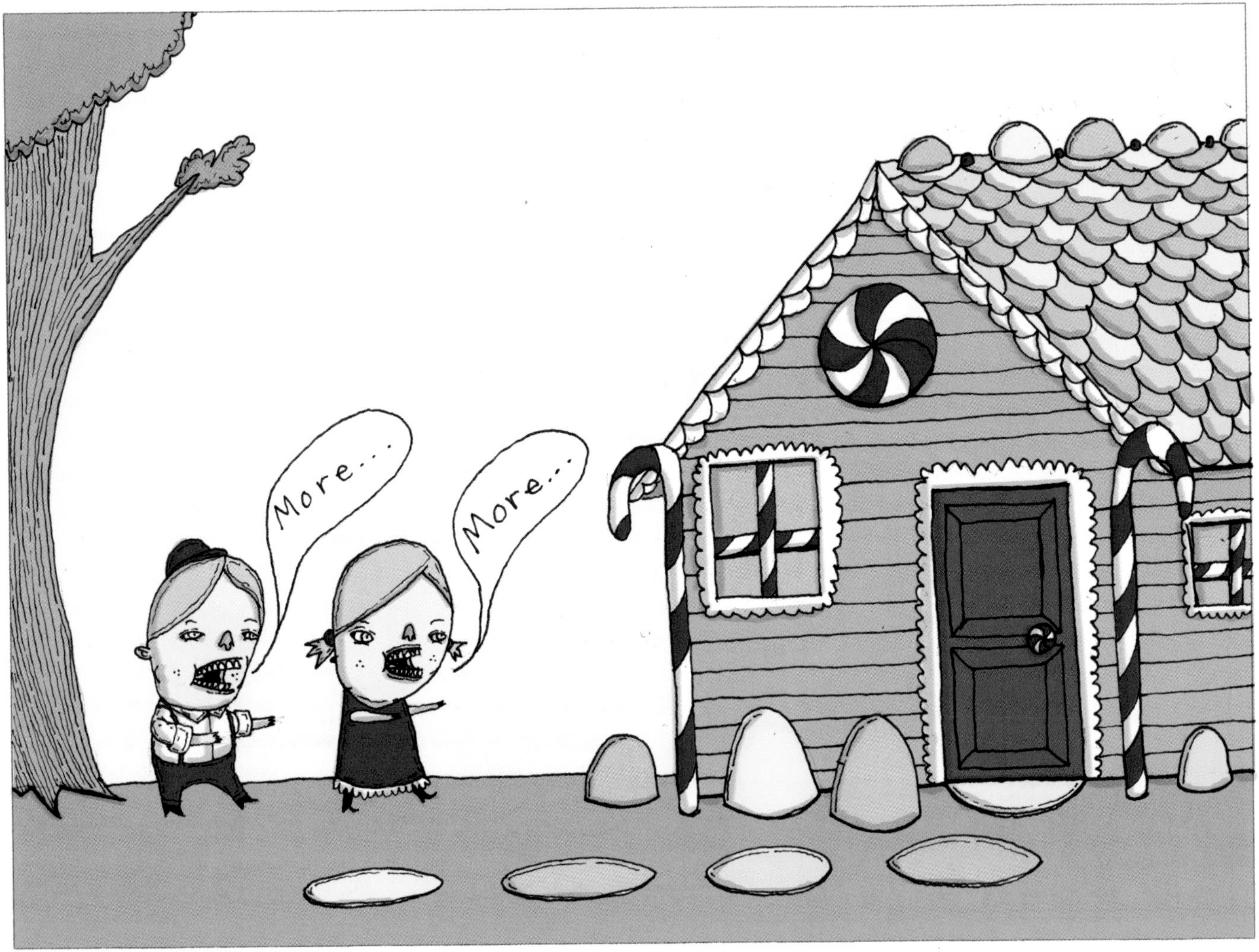
More...
More...

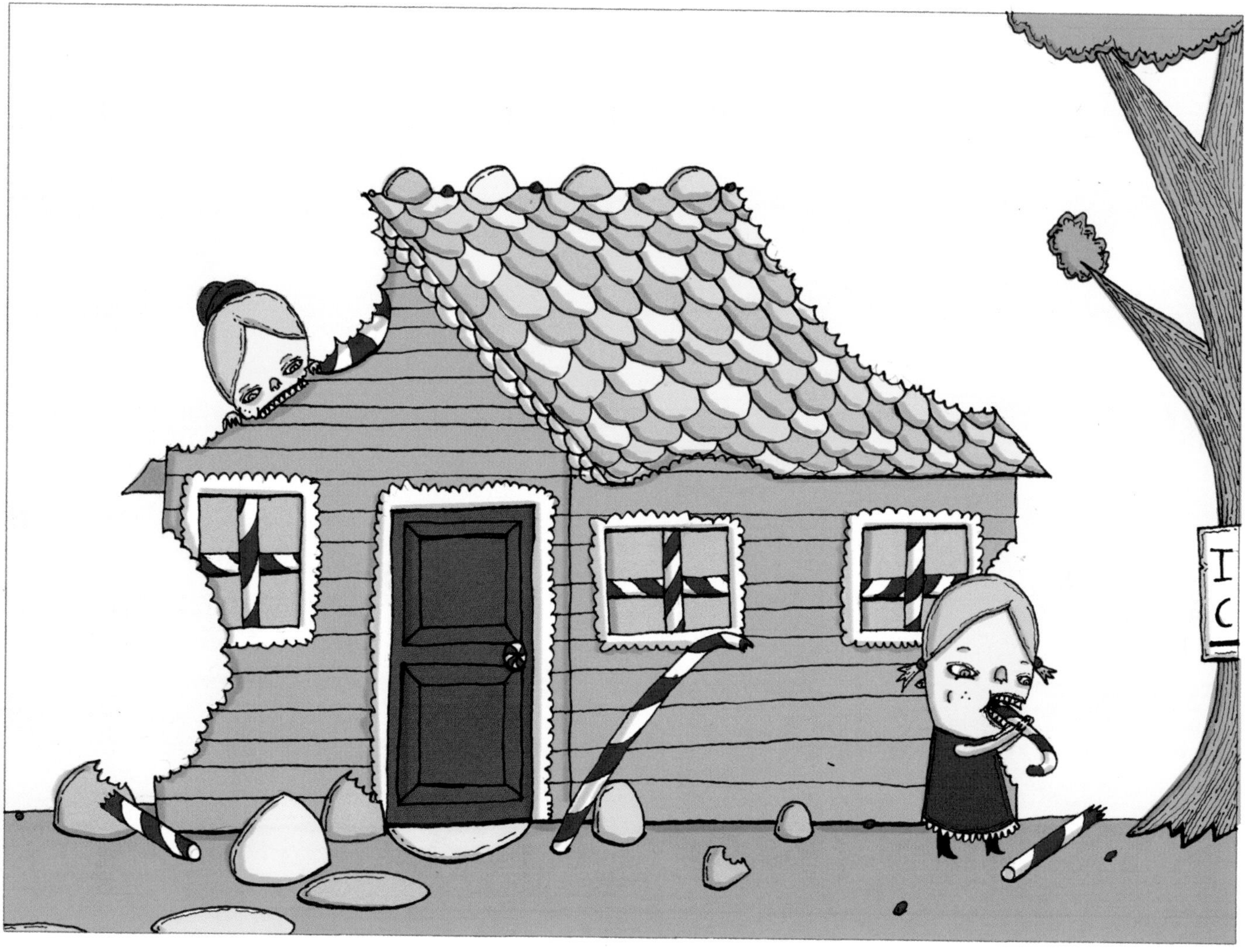

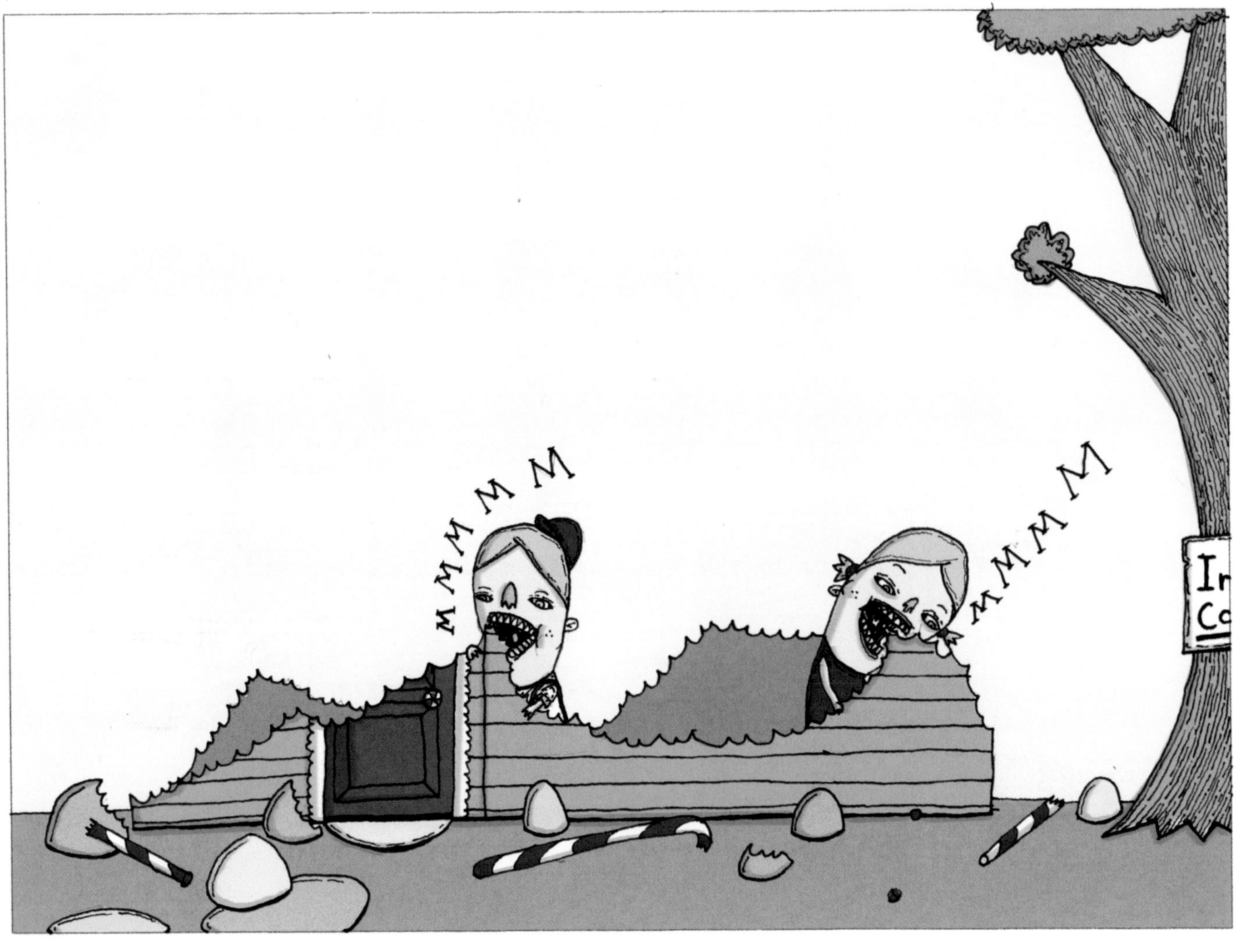
MMMMMM
MMMMMM

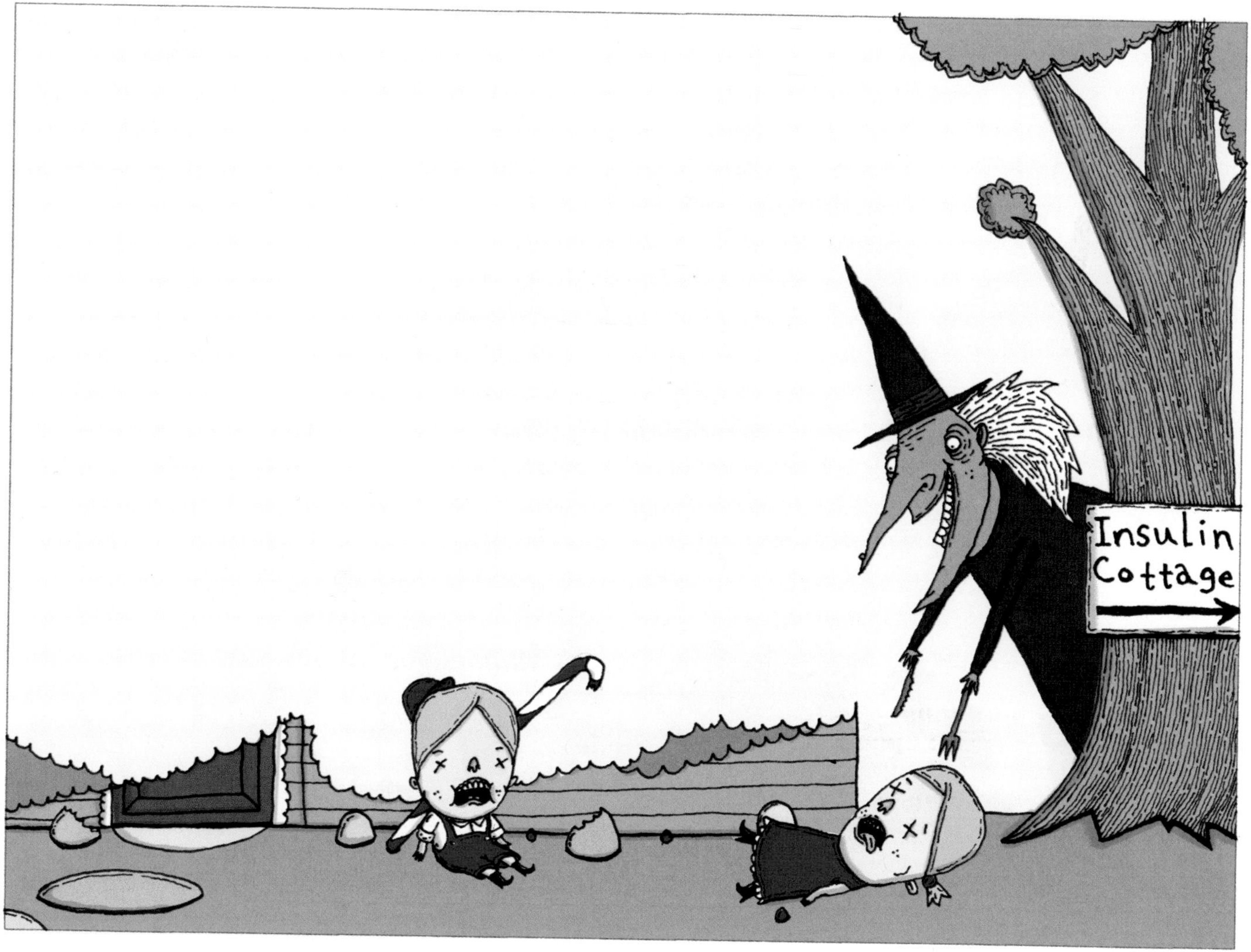
Insulin
Cottage

Over the Moon

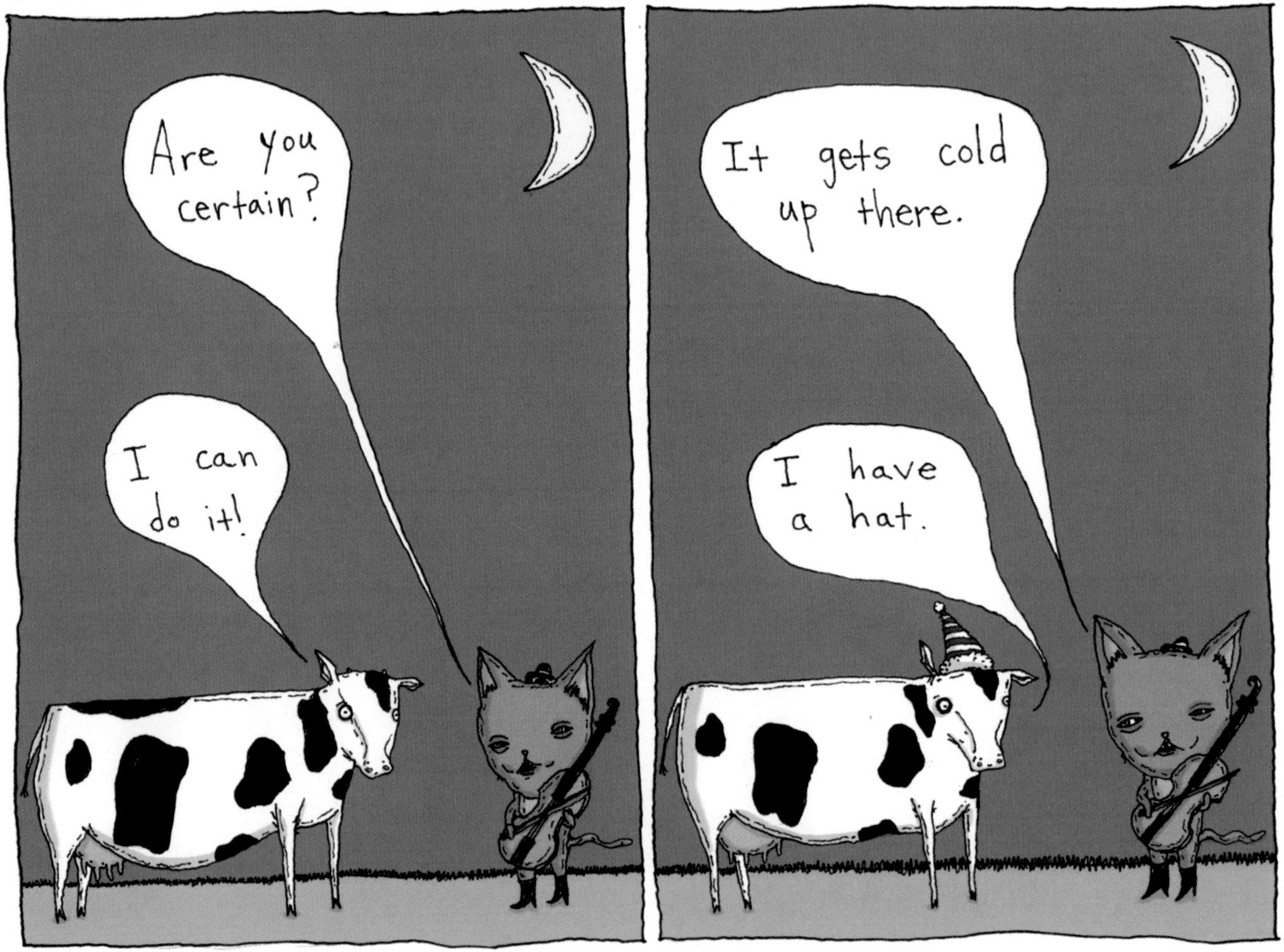
Are you certain?
I can do it!
It gets cold up there.
I have a hat.

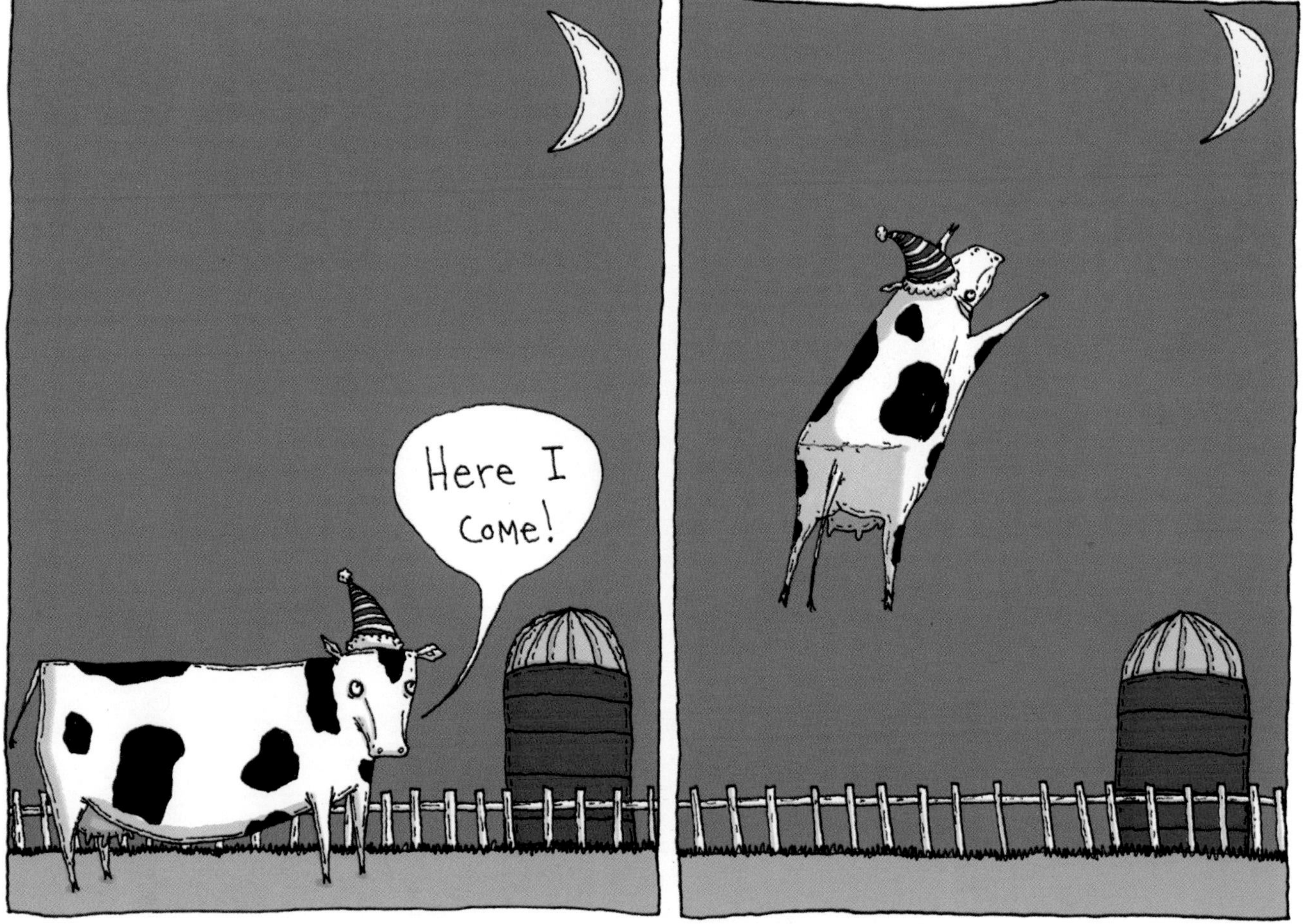
Here I come!

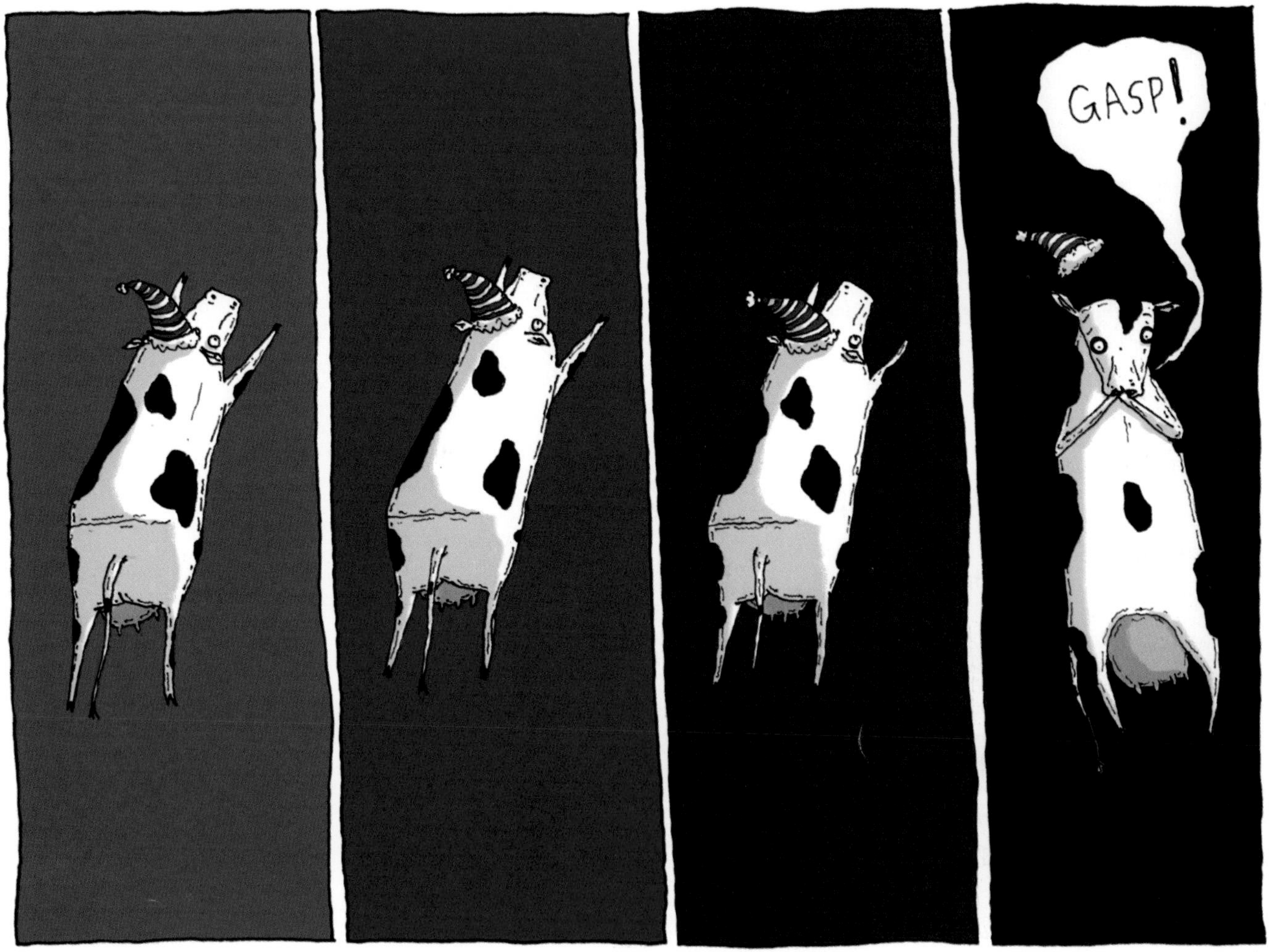
GASP!

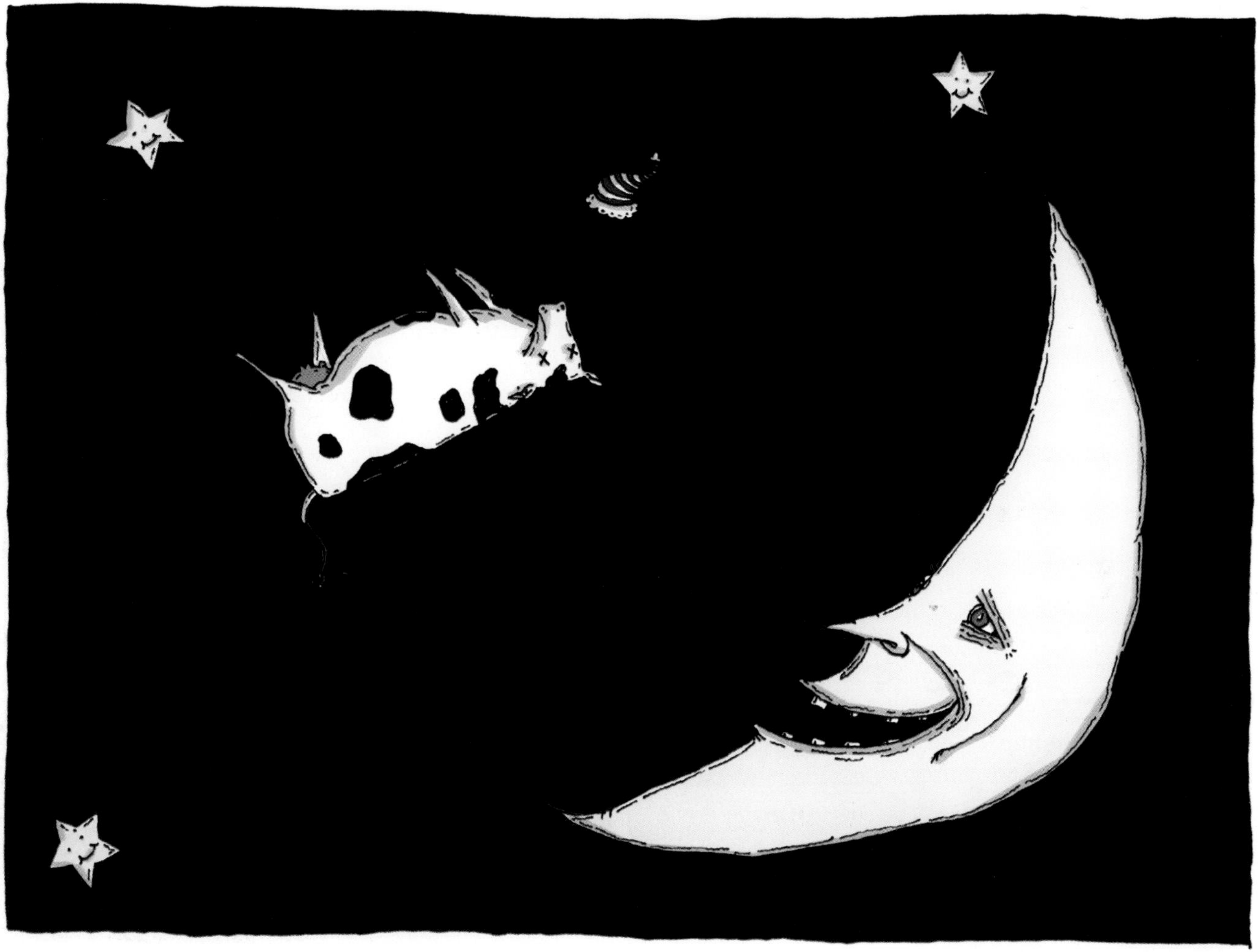

Humpty's Breakthrough

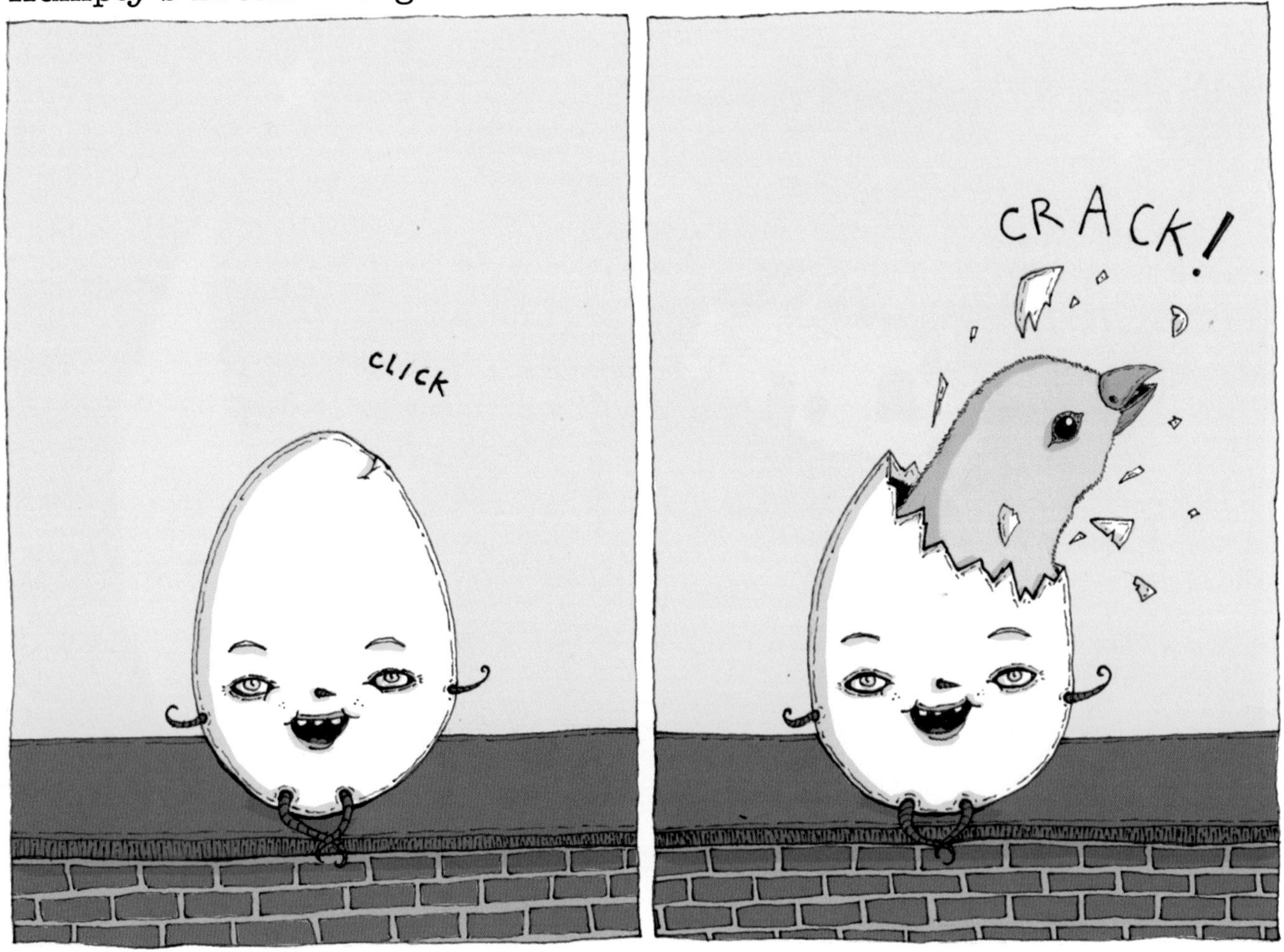
CLICK
CRACK!

Great Aquatic Romance #1

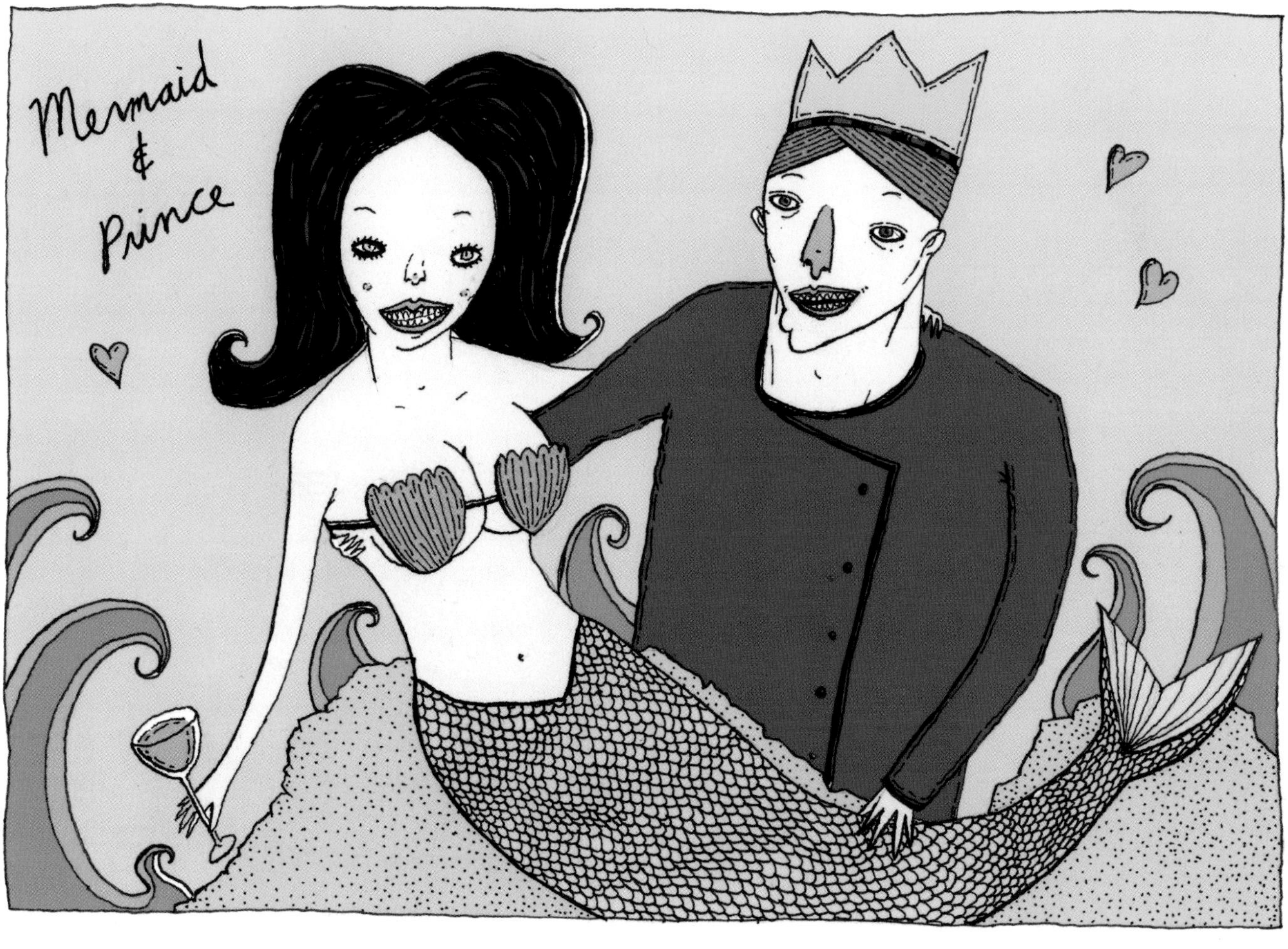
Mermaid
&
Prince

# The Ugly Truth

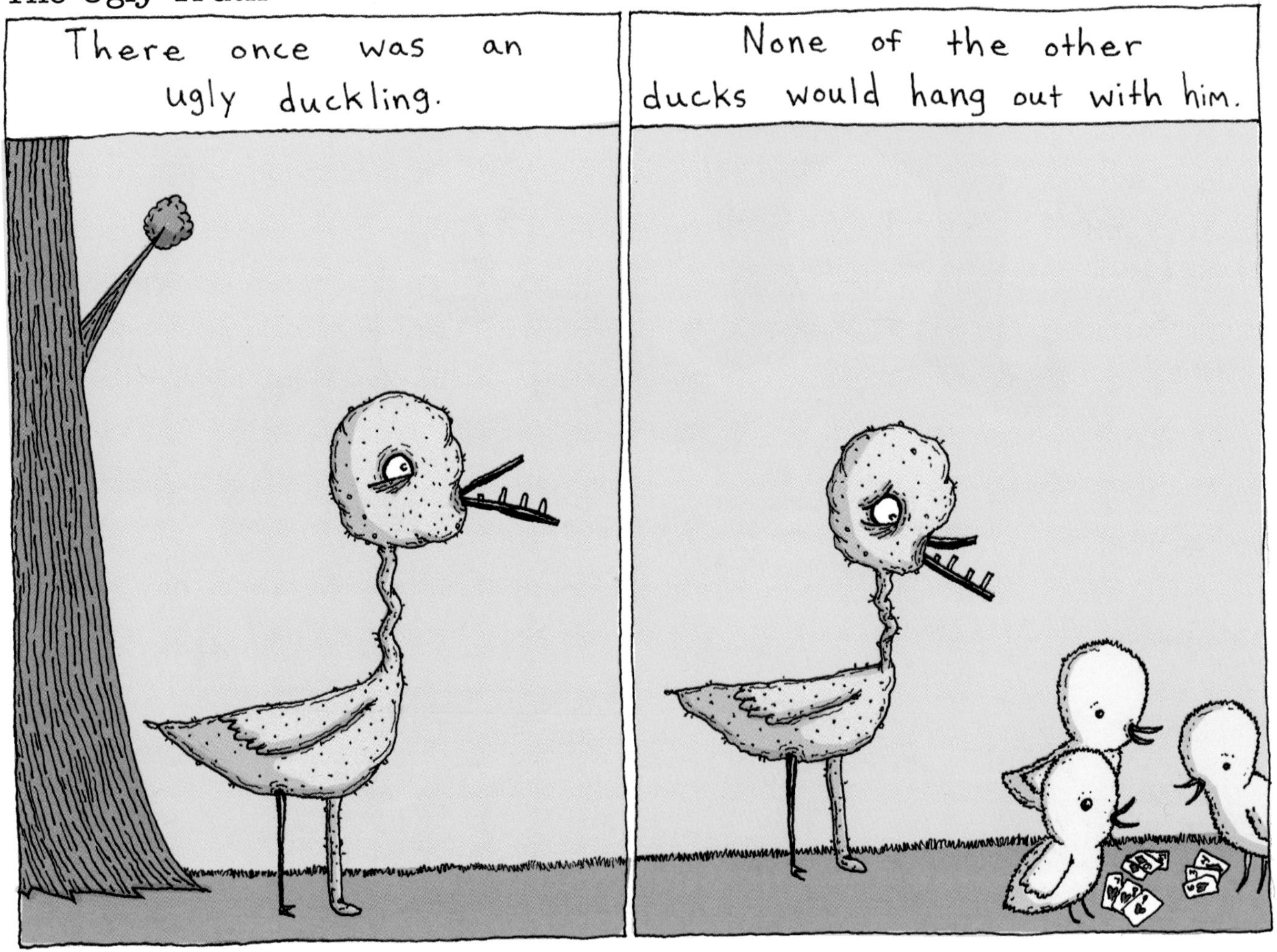
There once was an ugly duckling.
None of the other ducks would hang out with him.

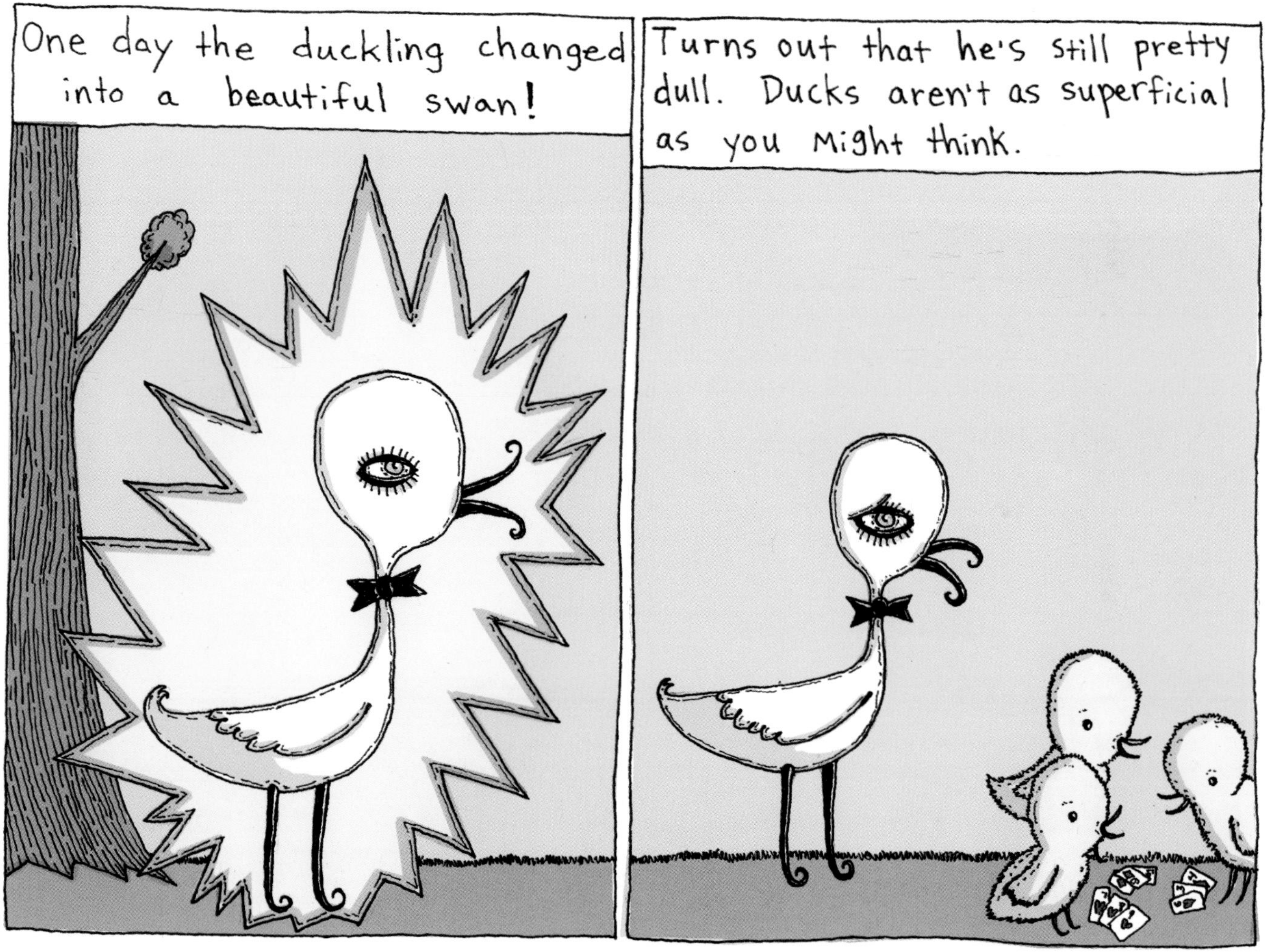
One day the duckling changed into a beautiful swan!
Turns out that he's still pretty dull. Ducks aren't as superficial as you might think.

Pinocchio's Nephew

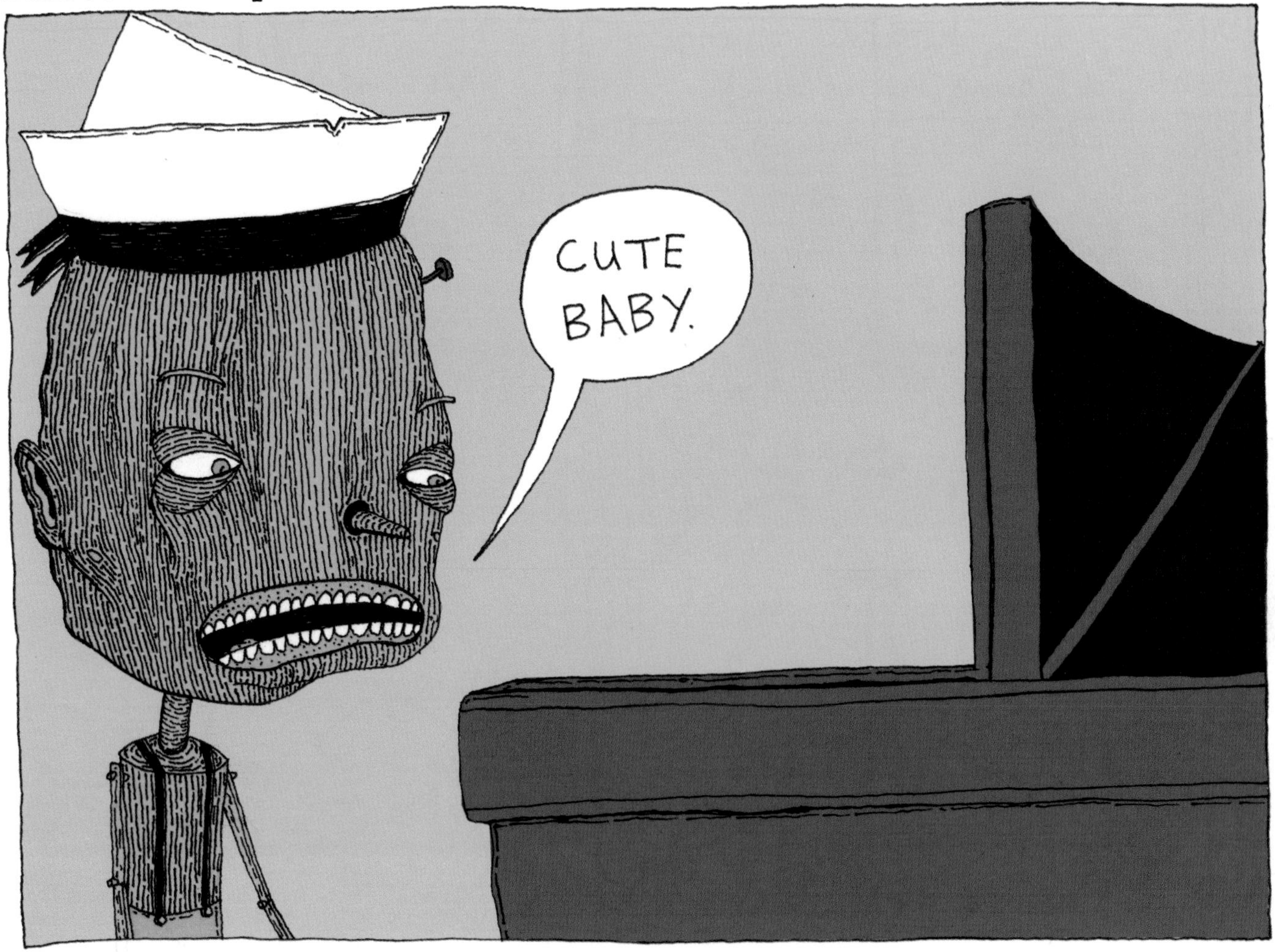
CUTE BABY.

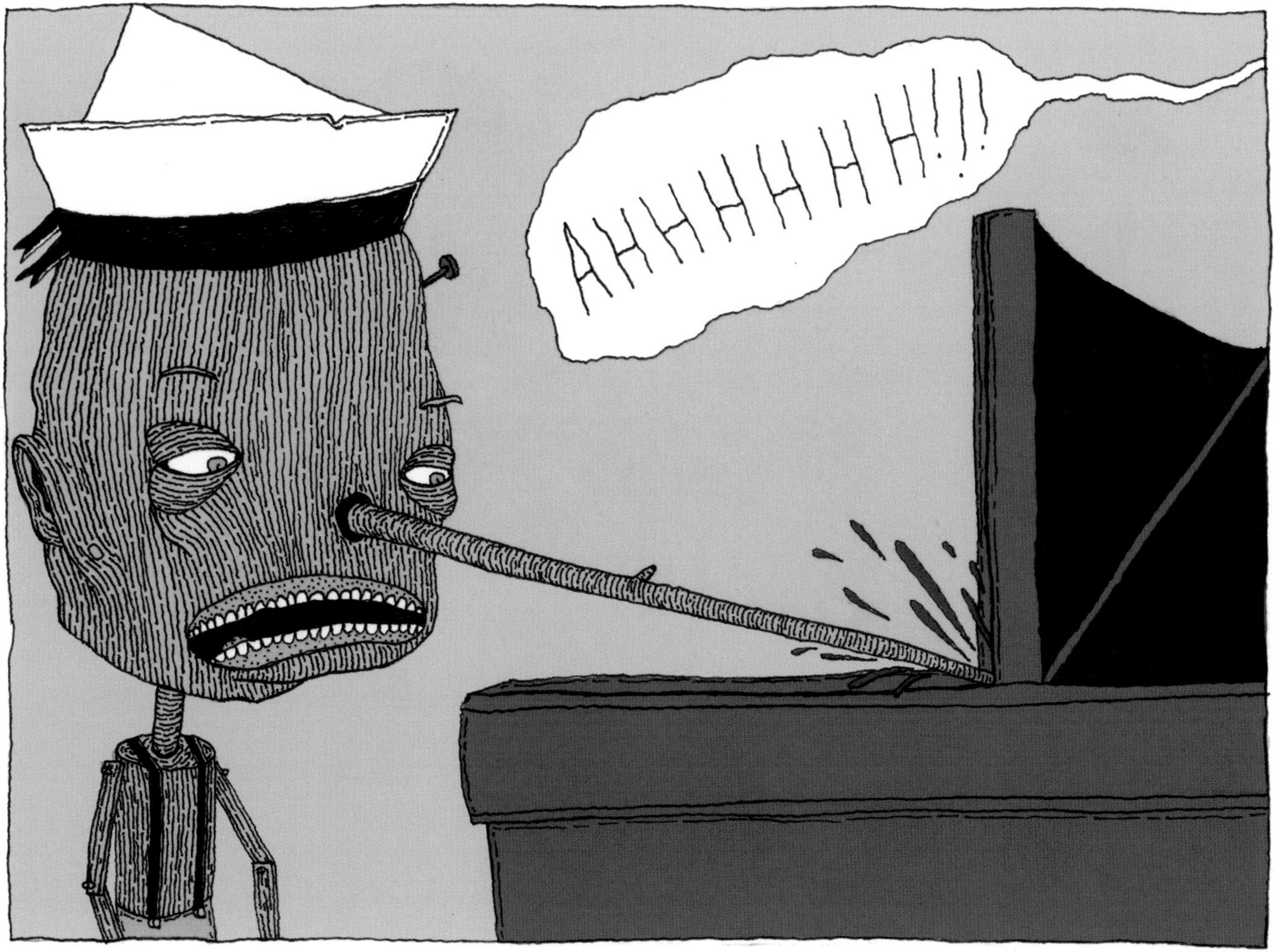
AHHHHHHH!!

The Hairy Situation

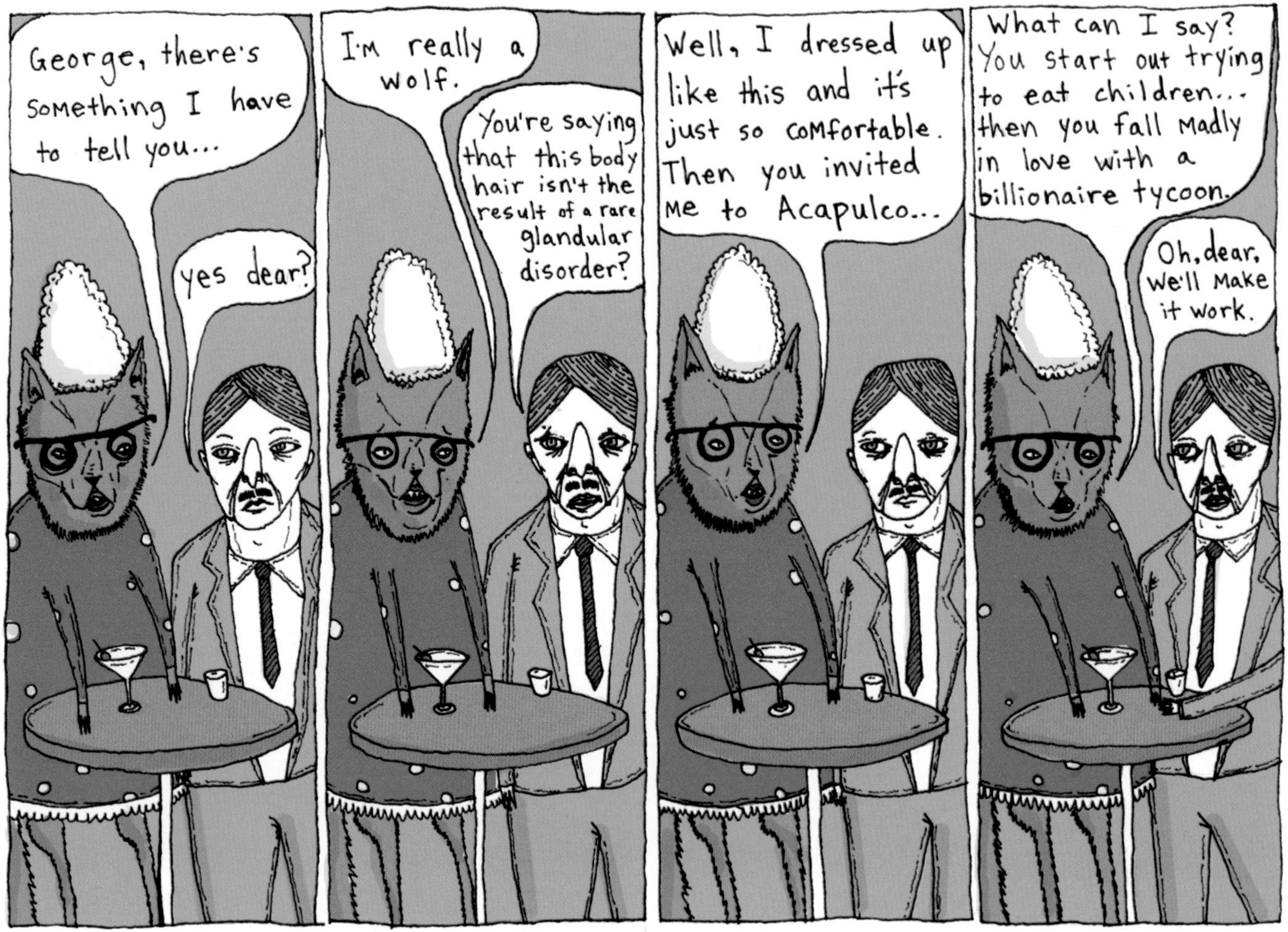
George, there's something I have to tell you...
yes dear?
I'm really a wolf.
You're saying that this body hair isn't the result of a rare glandular disorder?
Well, I dressed up like this and it's just so comfortable. Then you invited me to Acapulco...
What can I say? You start out trying to eat children... then you fall madly in love with a billionaire tycoon.
Oh, dear, we'll make it work.

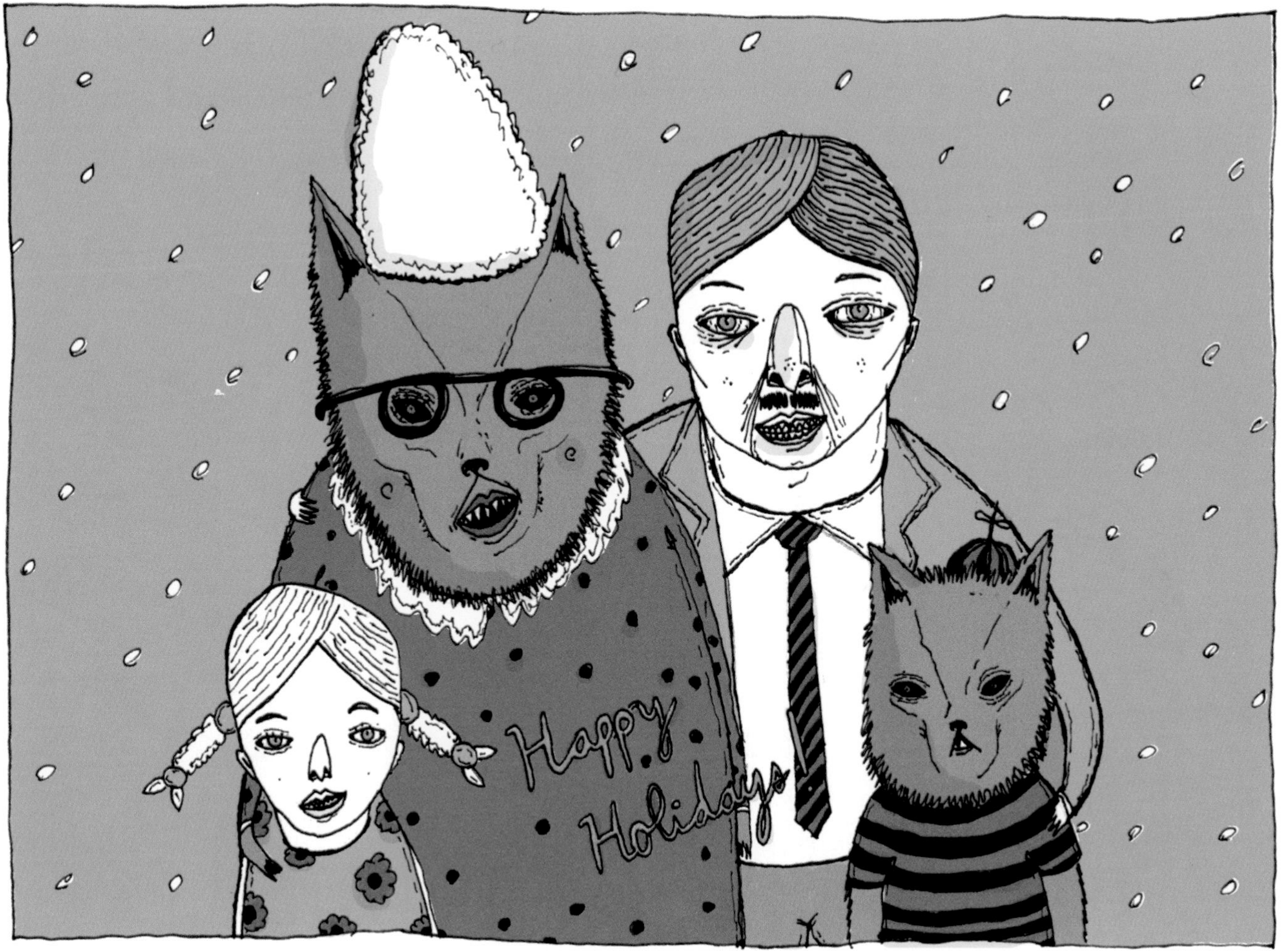
Happy Holidays!

Over Easy

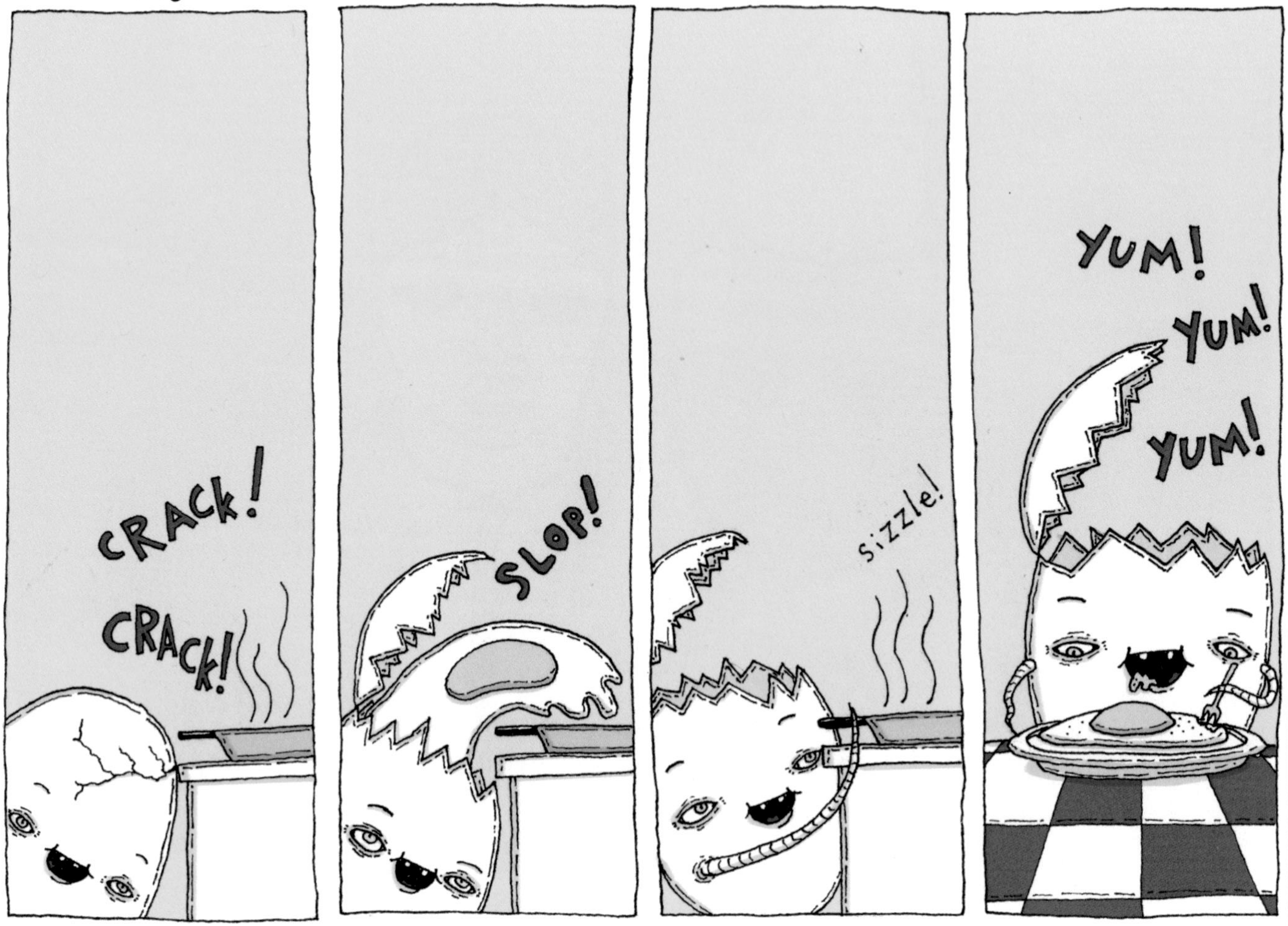
CRACK!
CRACK!
SLOP!
sizzle!
YUM!
YUM!
YUM!

Great Aquatic Romance #2

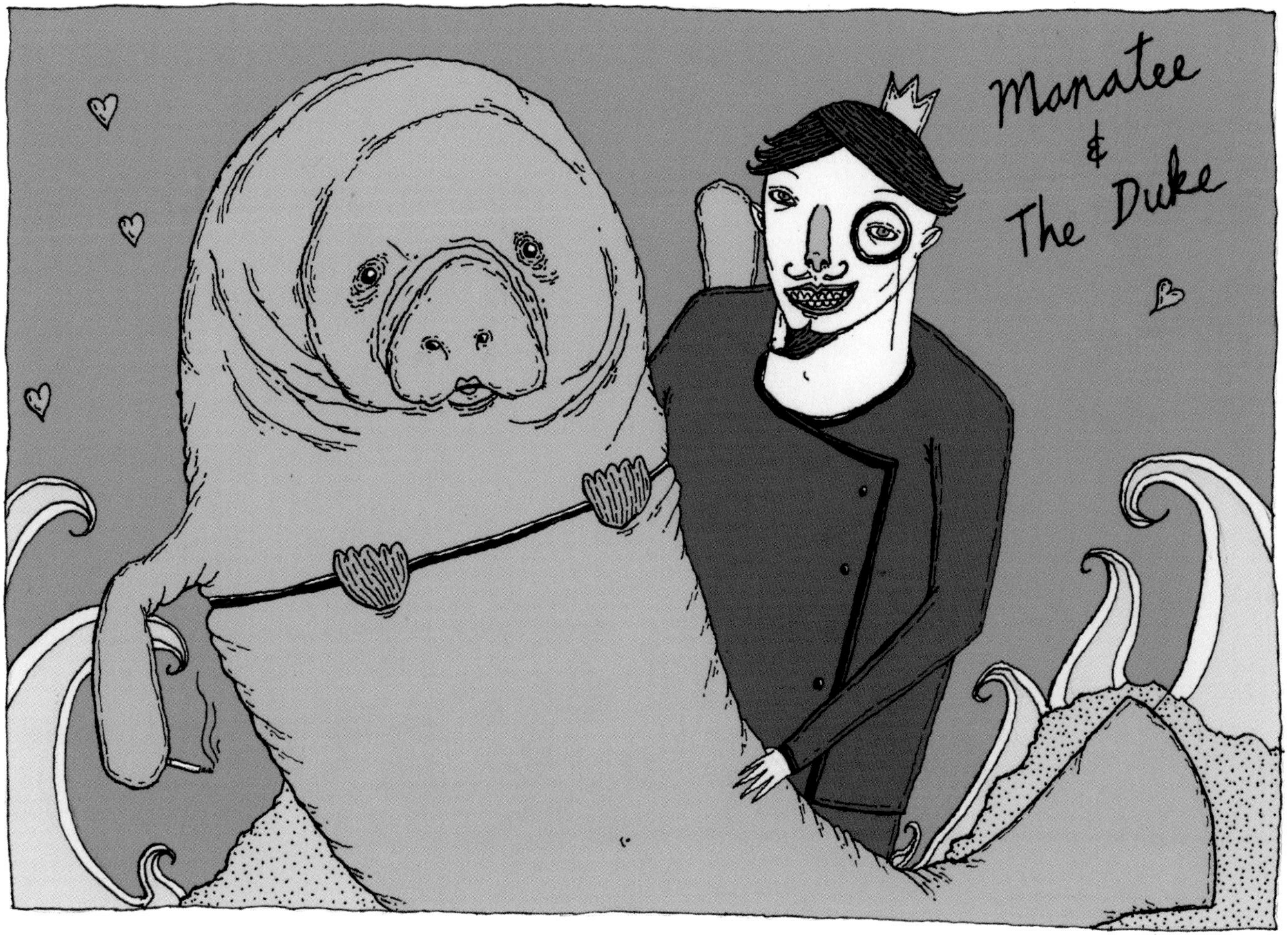
Manatee
&
The Duke

Sleeping Beauty

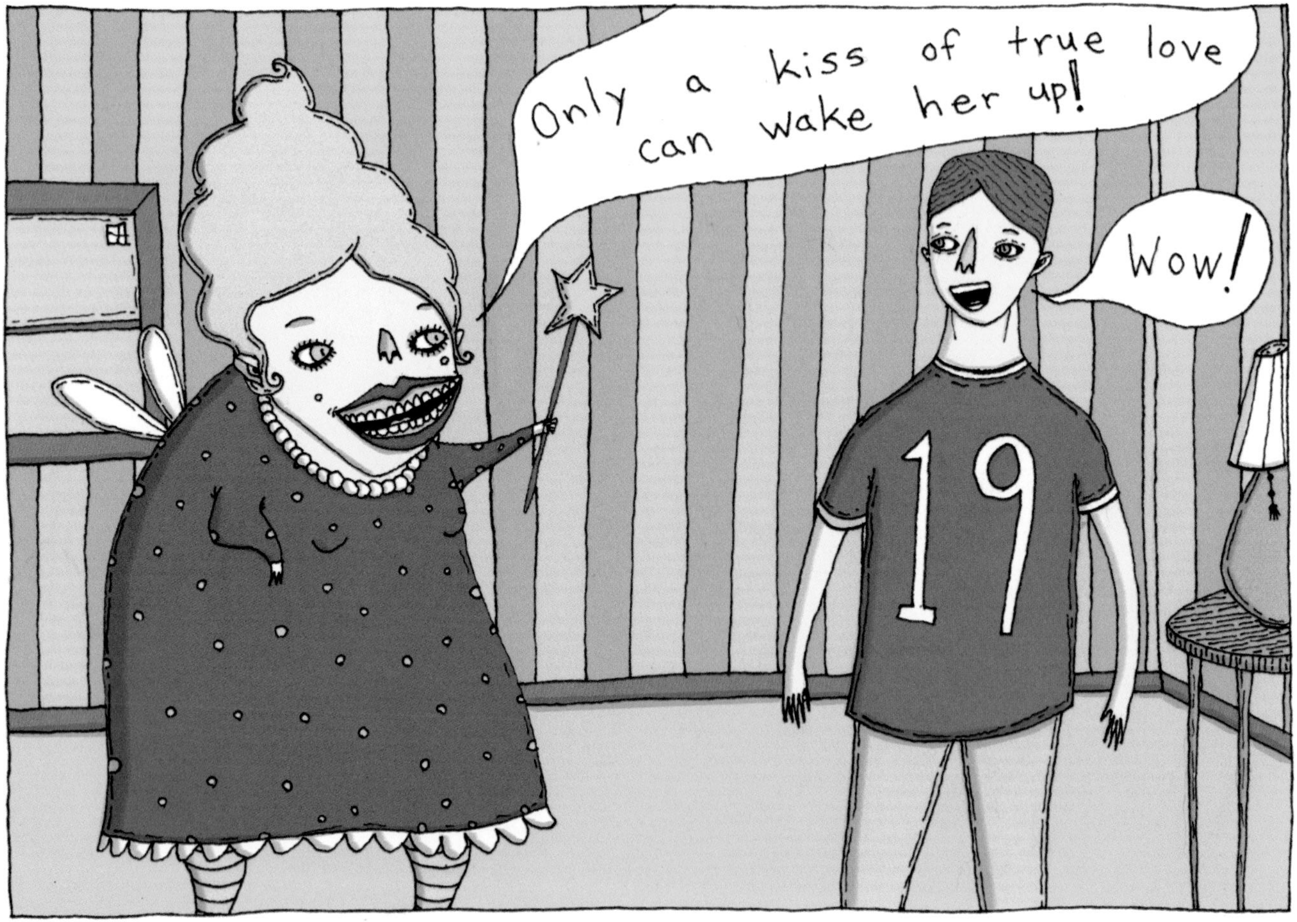
Only a kiss of true love can wake her up!
Wow!

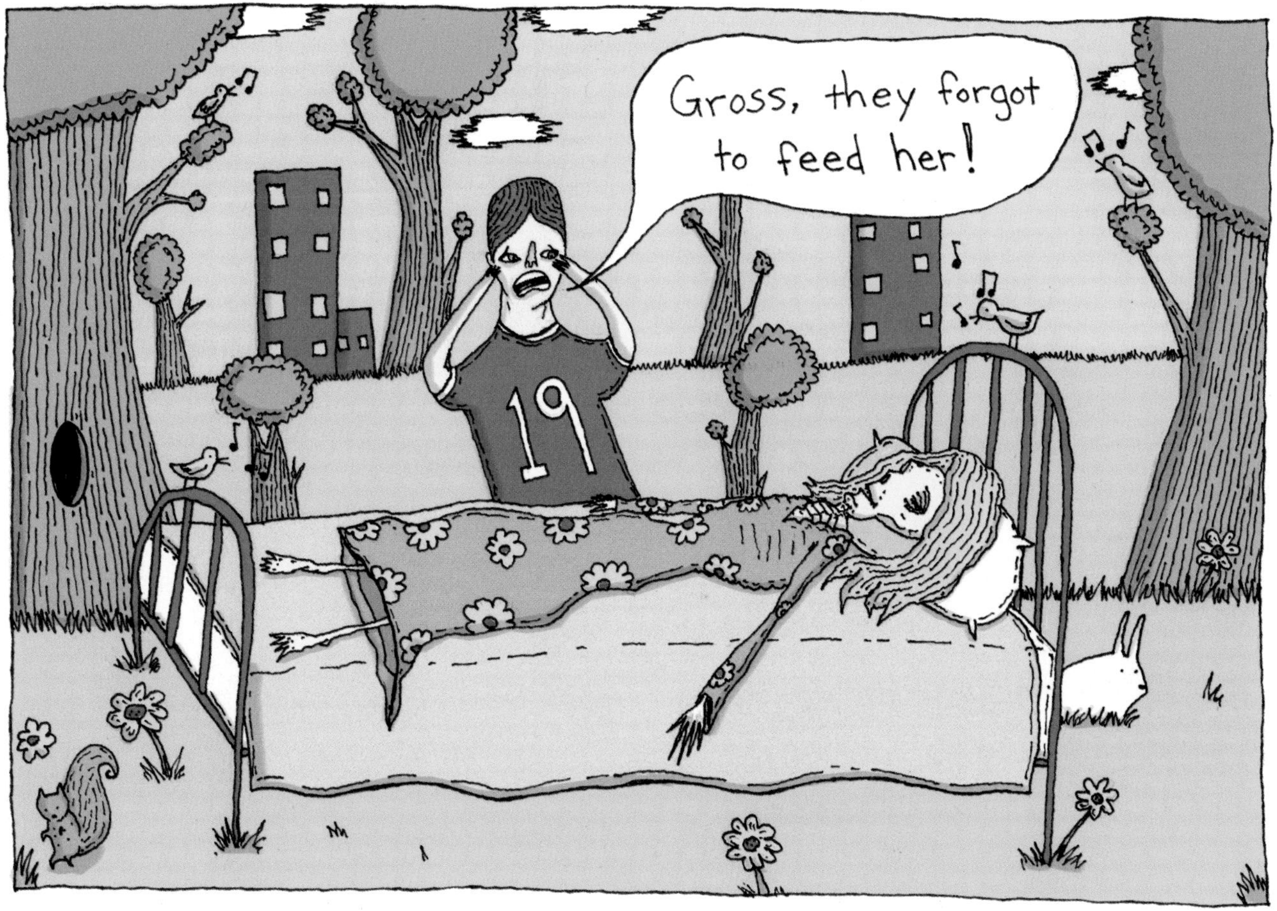
Gross, they forgot to feed her!
19

Pinocchio's Dummy

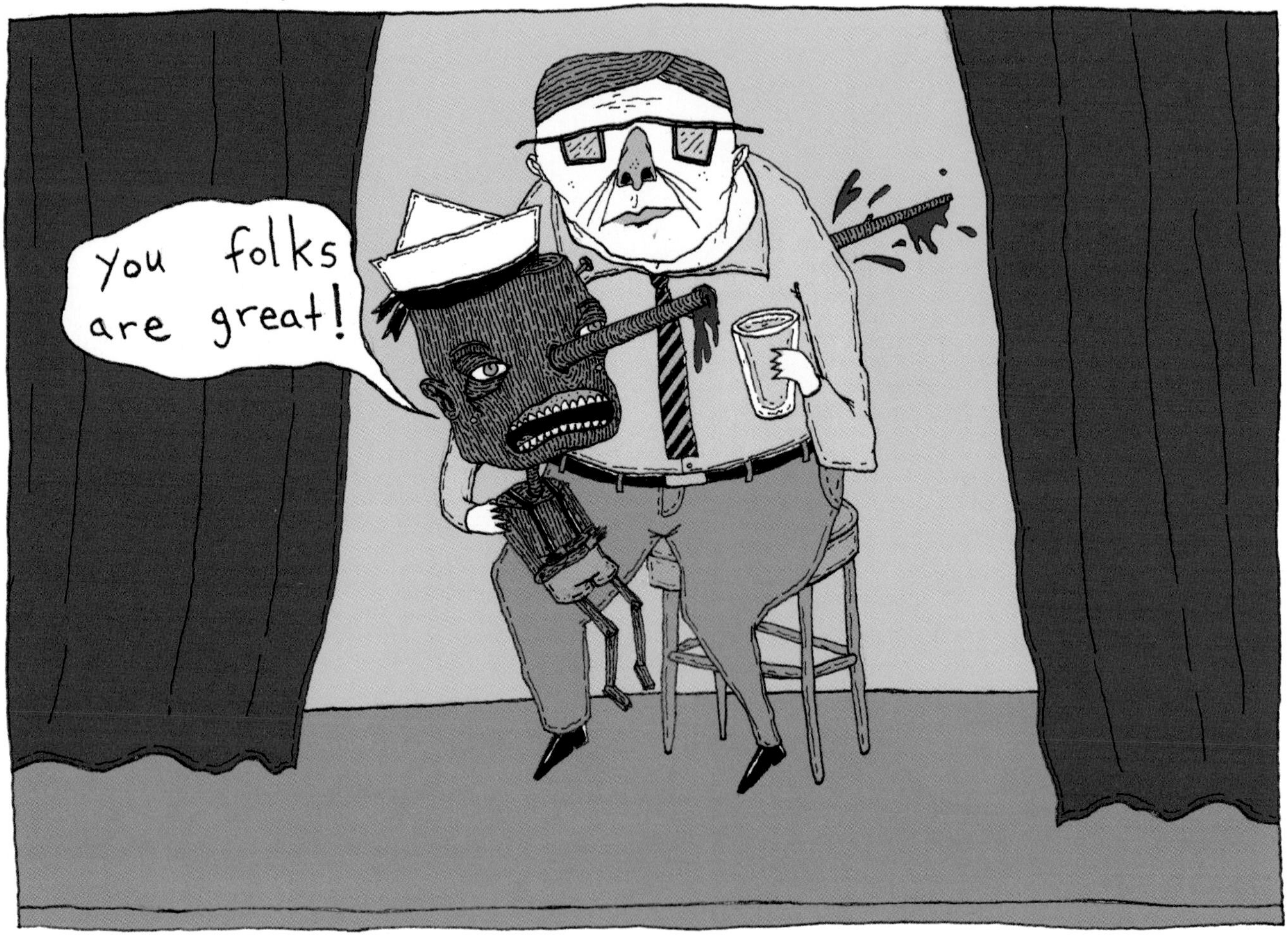
you folks are great!

# Big Manly Scent

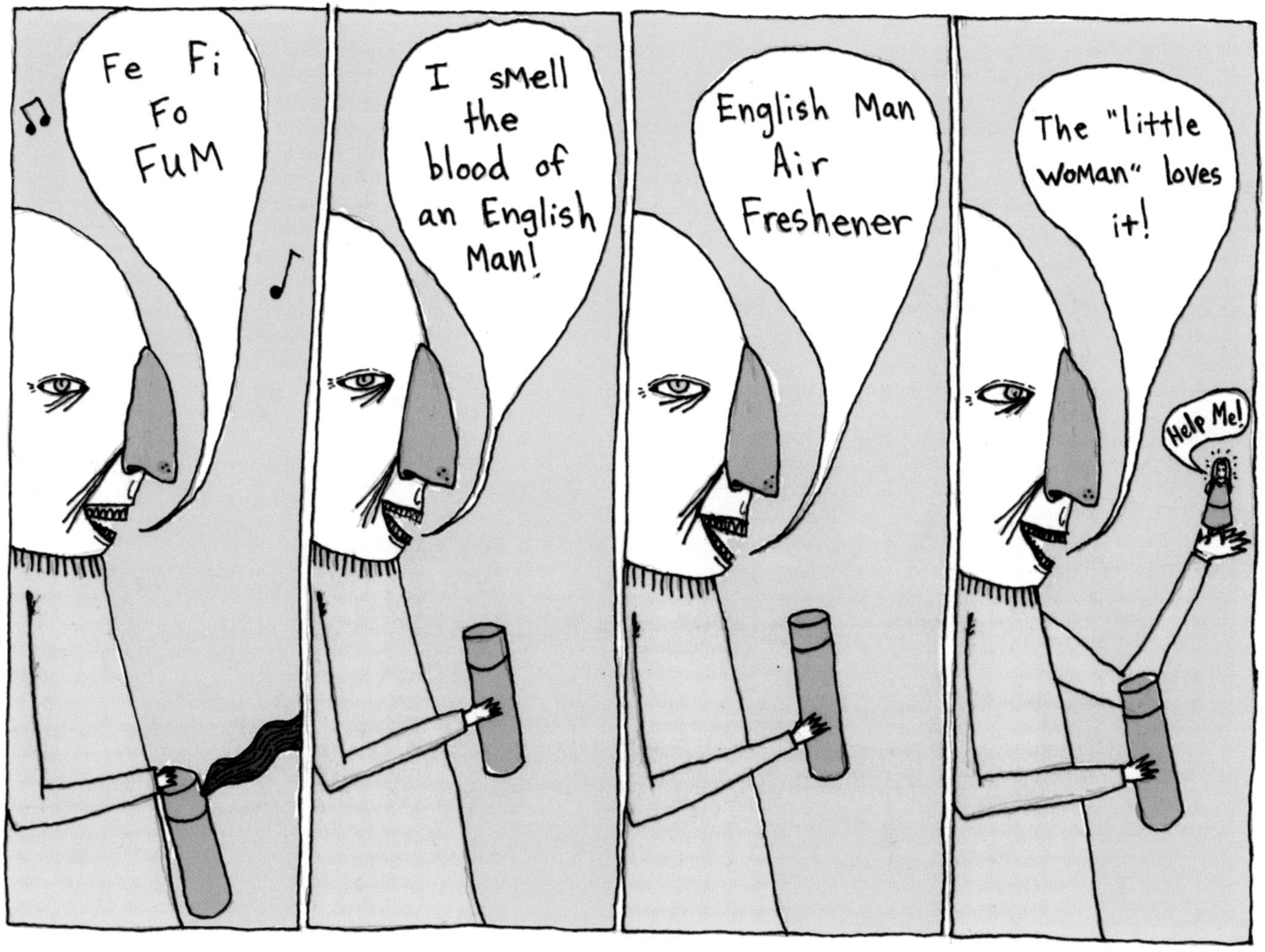
Fe Fi Fo FuM
I sMell the blood of an English Man!
English Man Air Freshener
The "little woMan" loves it!
Help Me!

Ham-fisted Justice

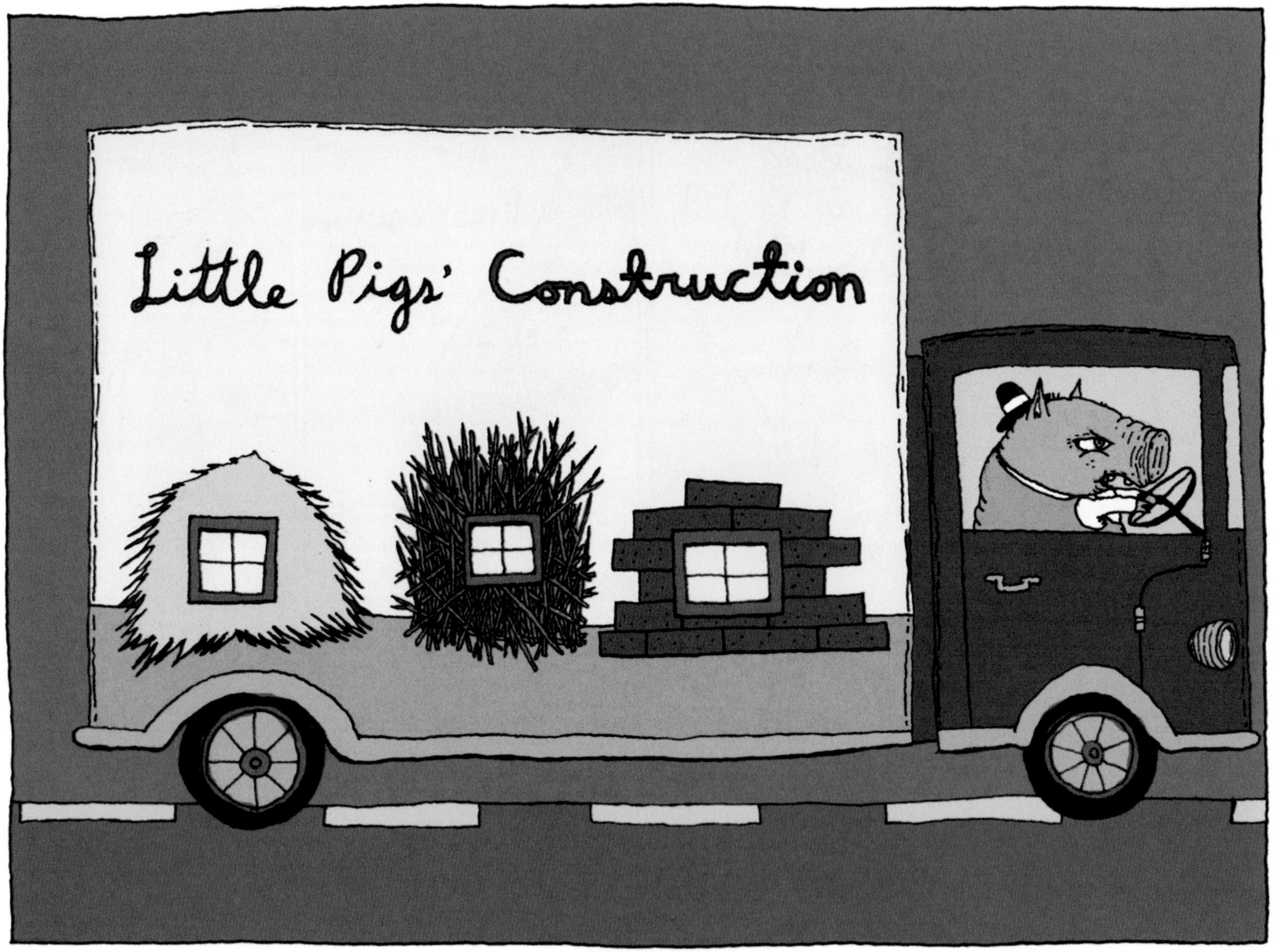
Little Pigs' Construction

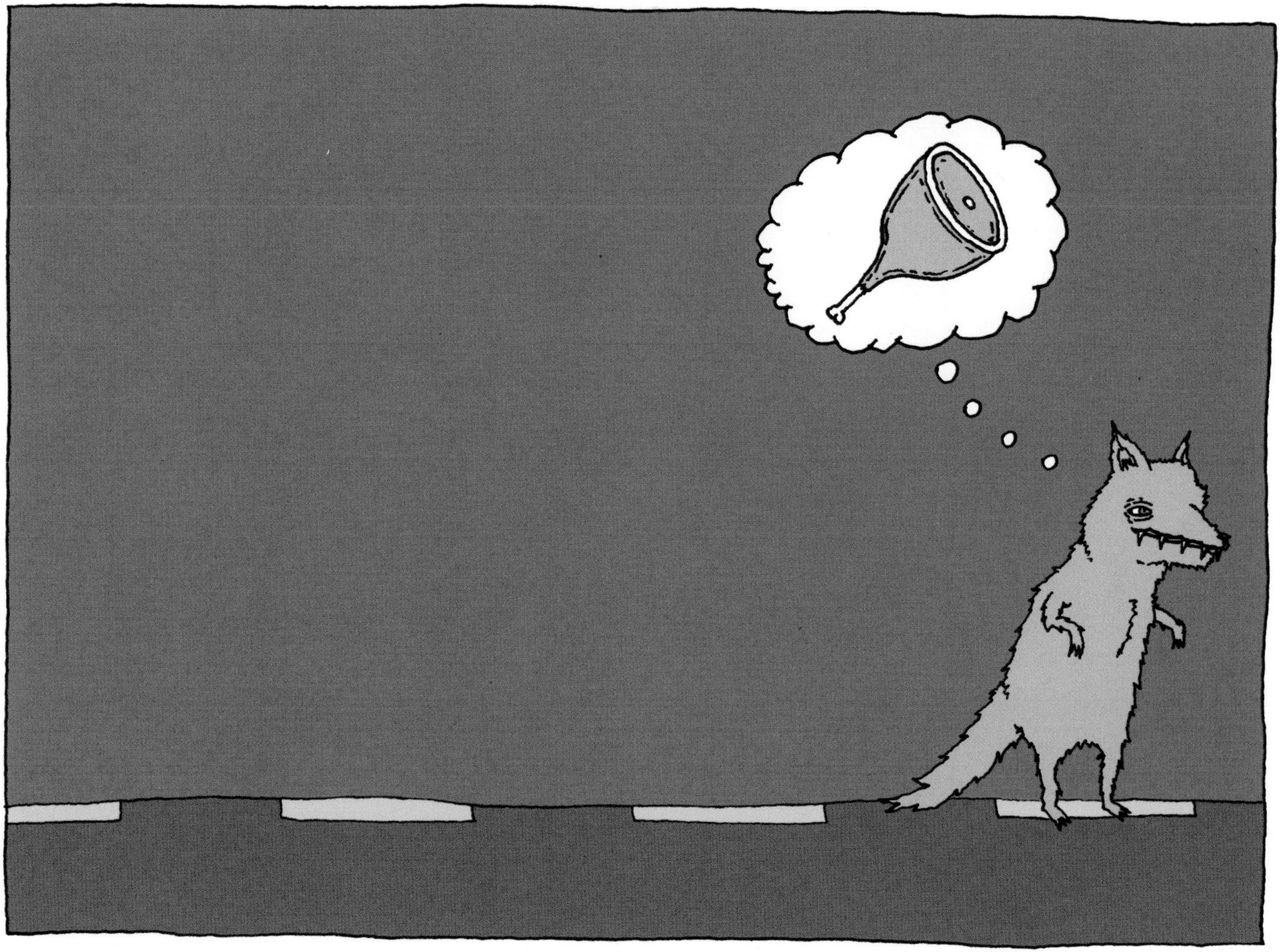

## Use the Stairs

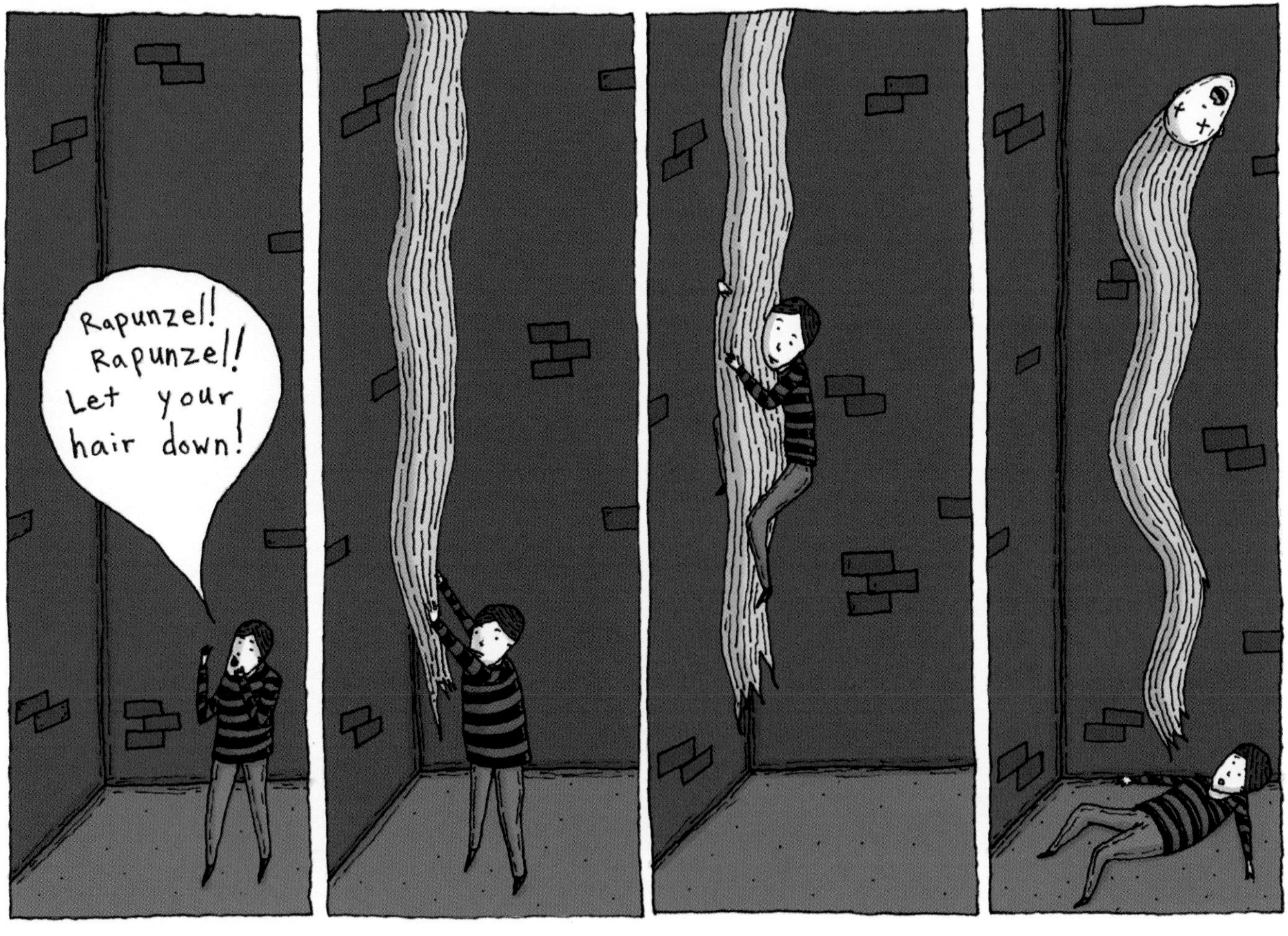
Rapunzel! Rapunzel! Let your hair down!

Blind Luck

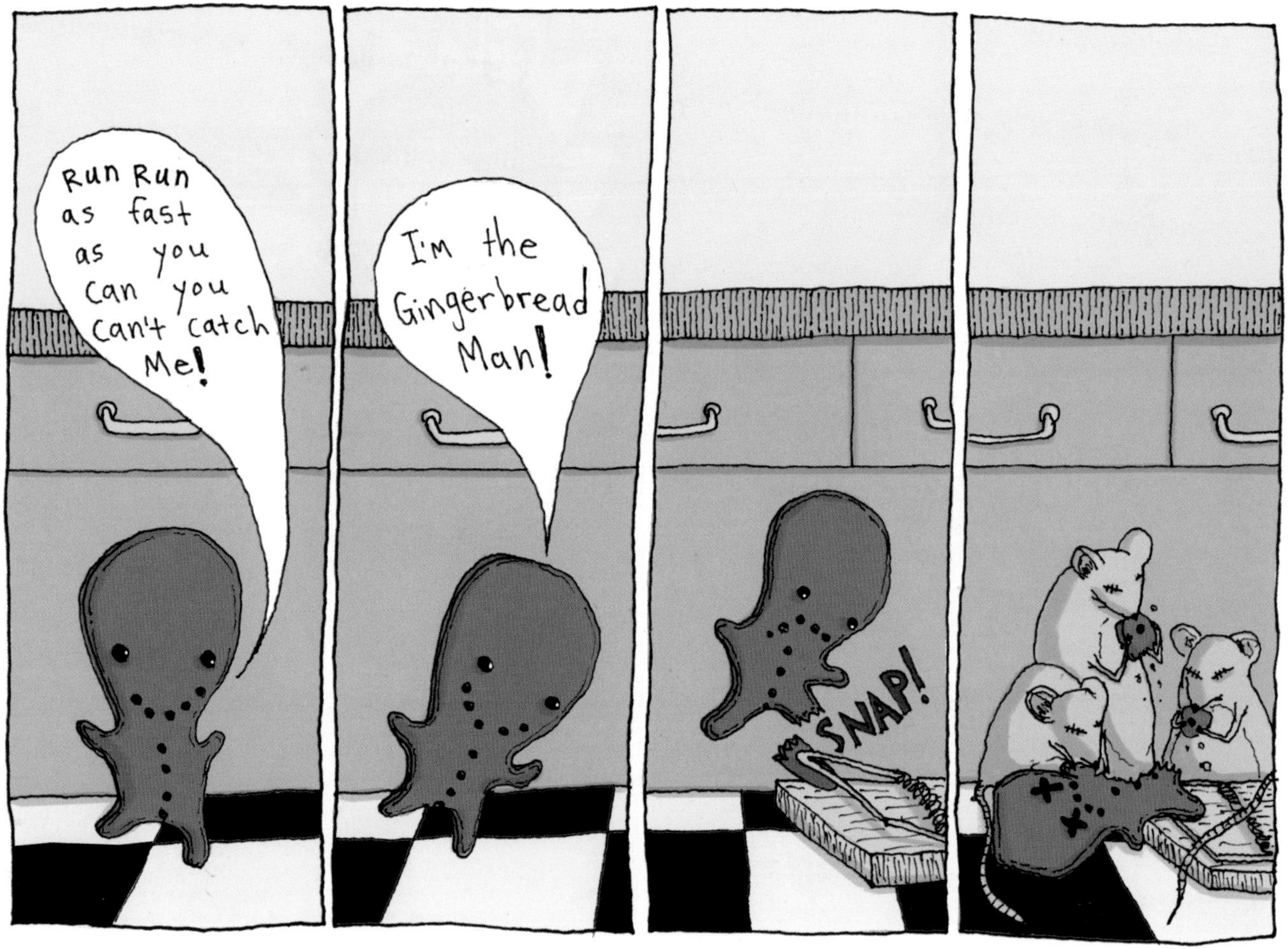
Run Run as fast as you can you can't catch Me!
I'm the Gingerbread Man!
SNAP!

French Kiss

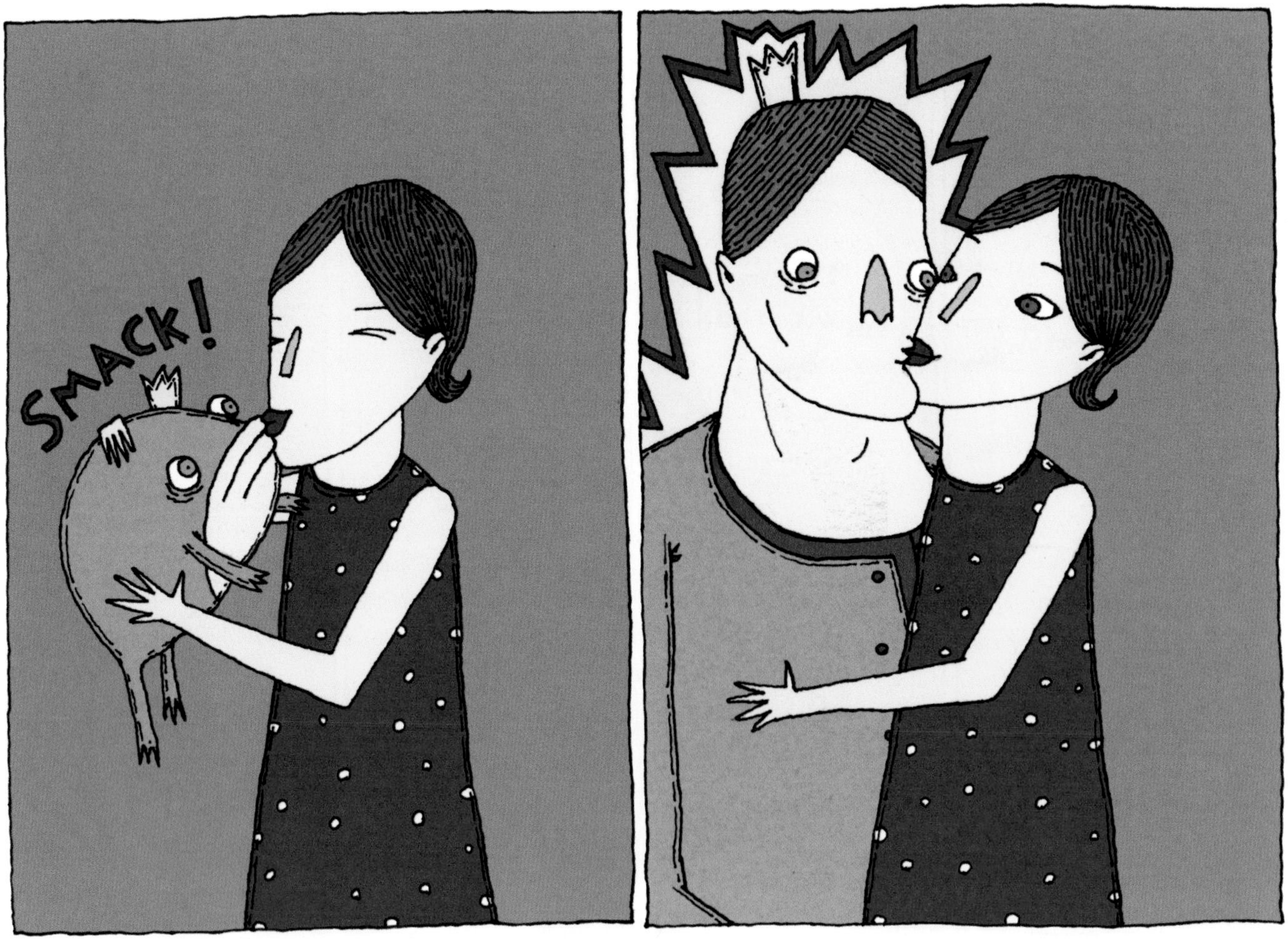
SMACK!

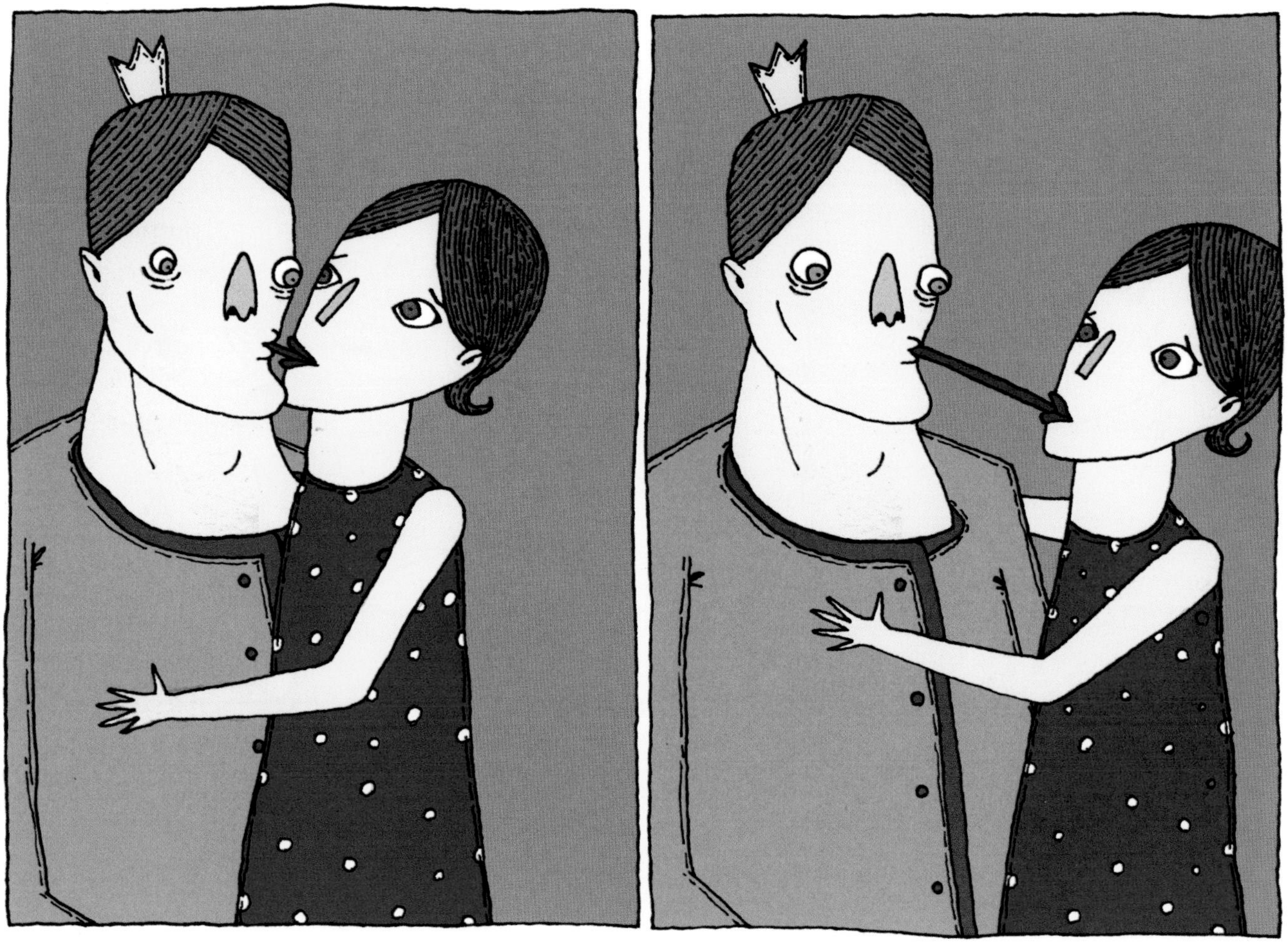

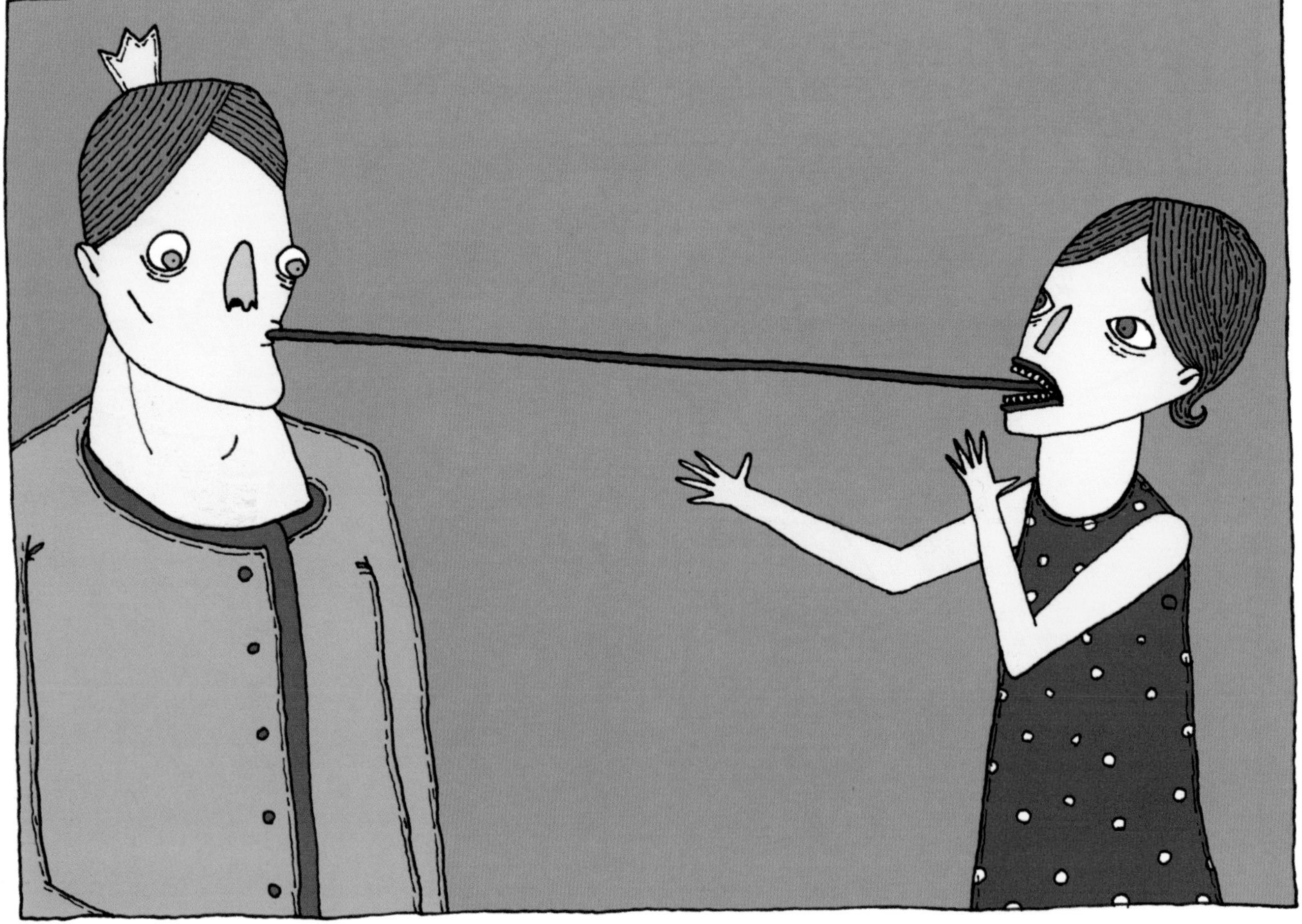

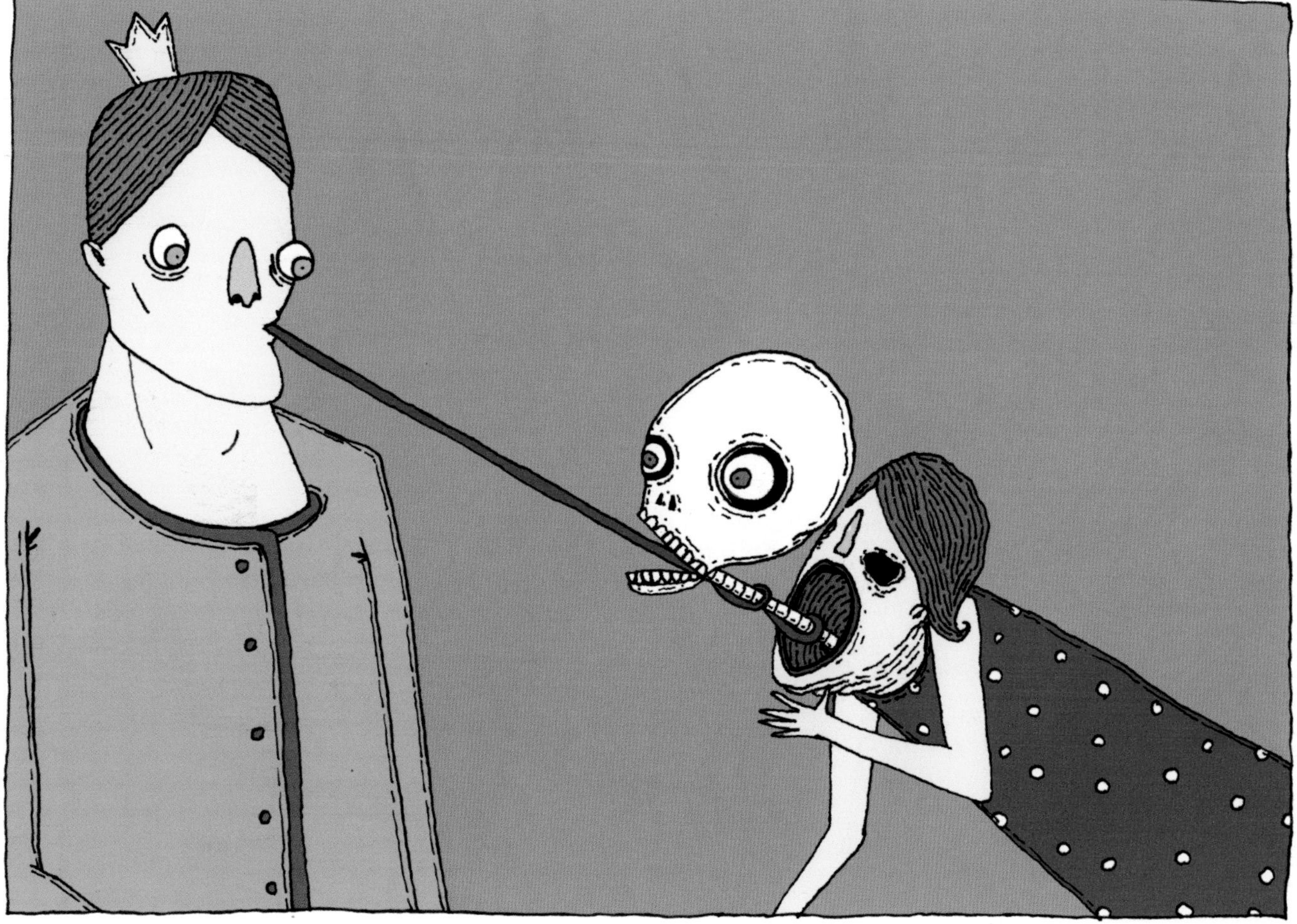

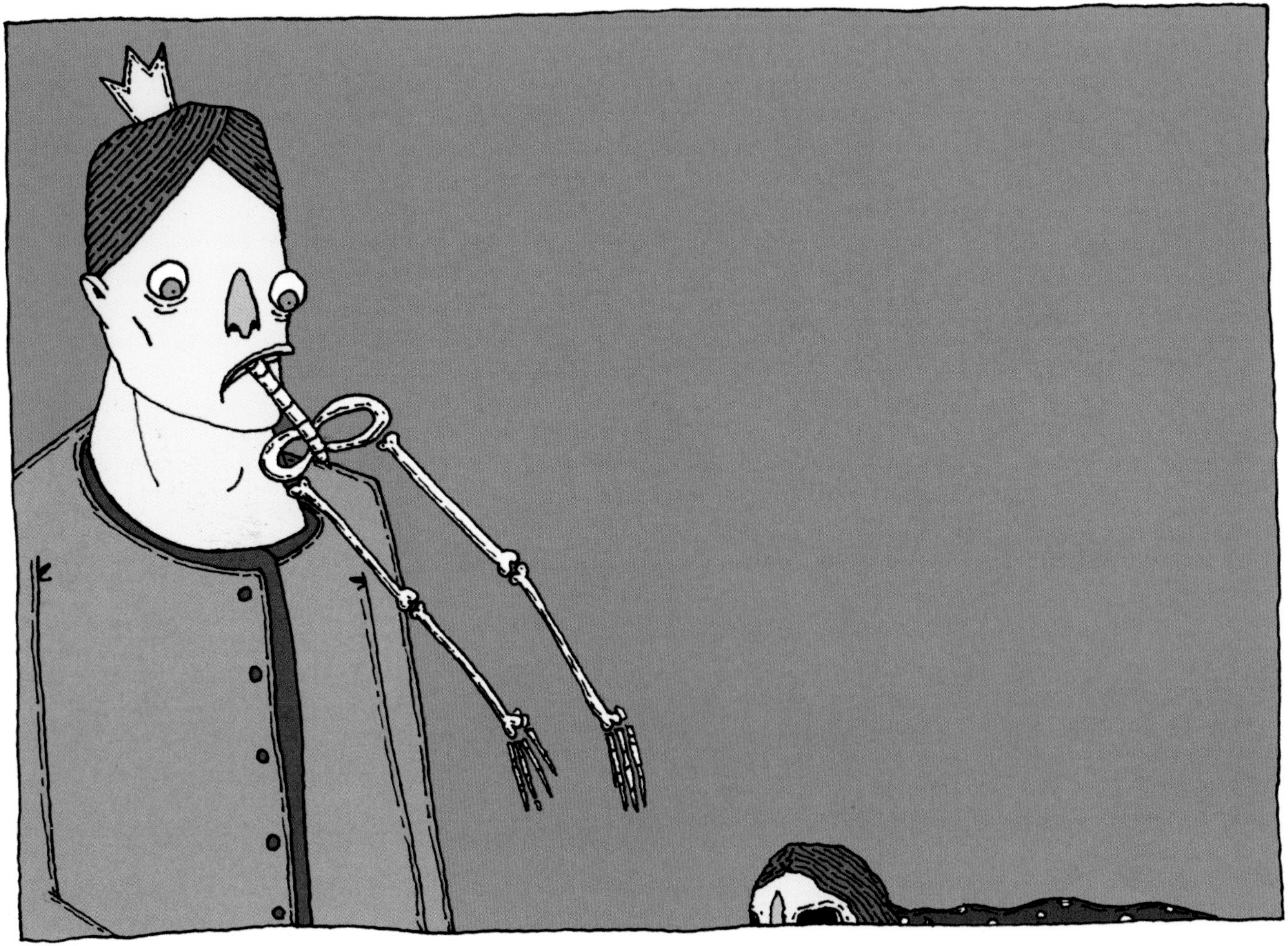

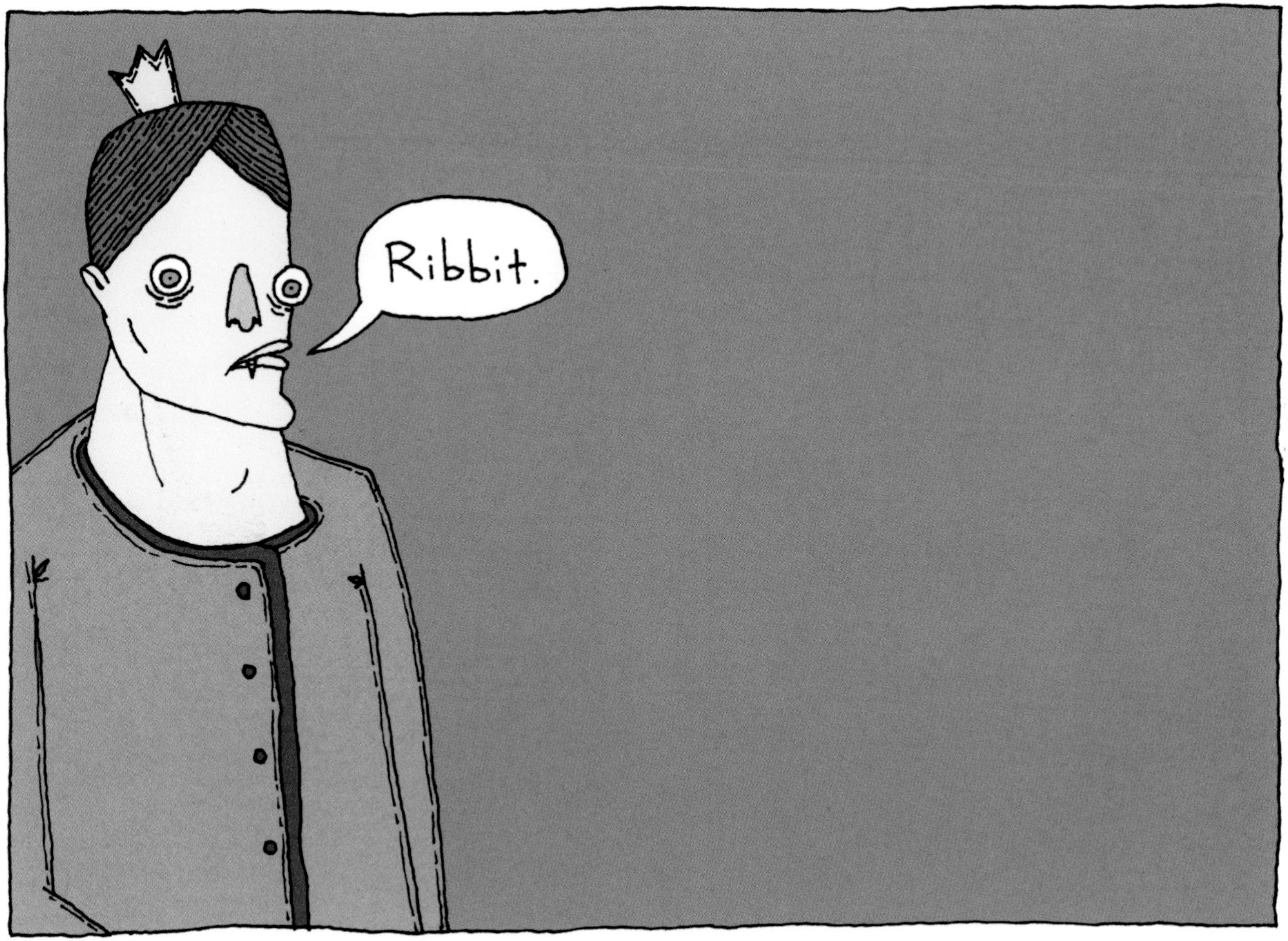
Ribbit.

Perfect Match

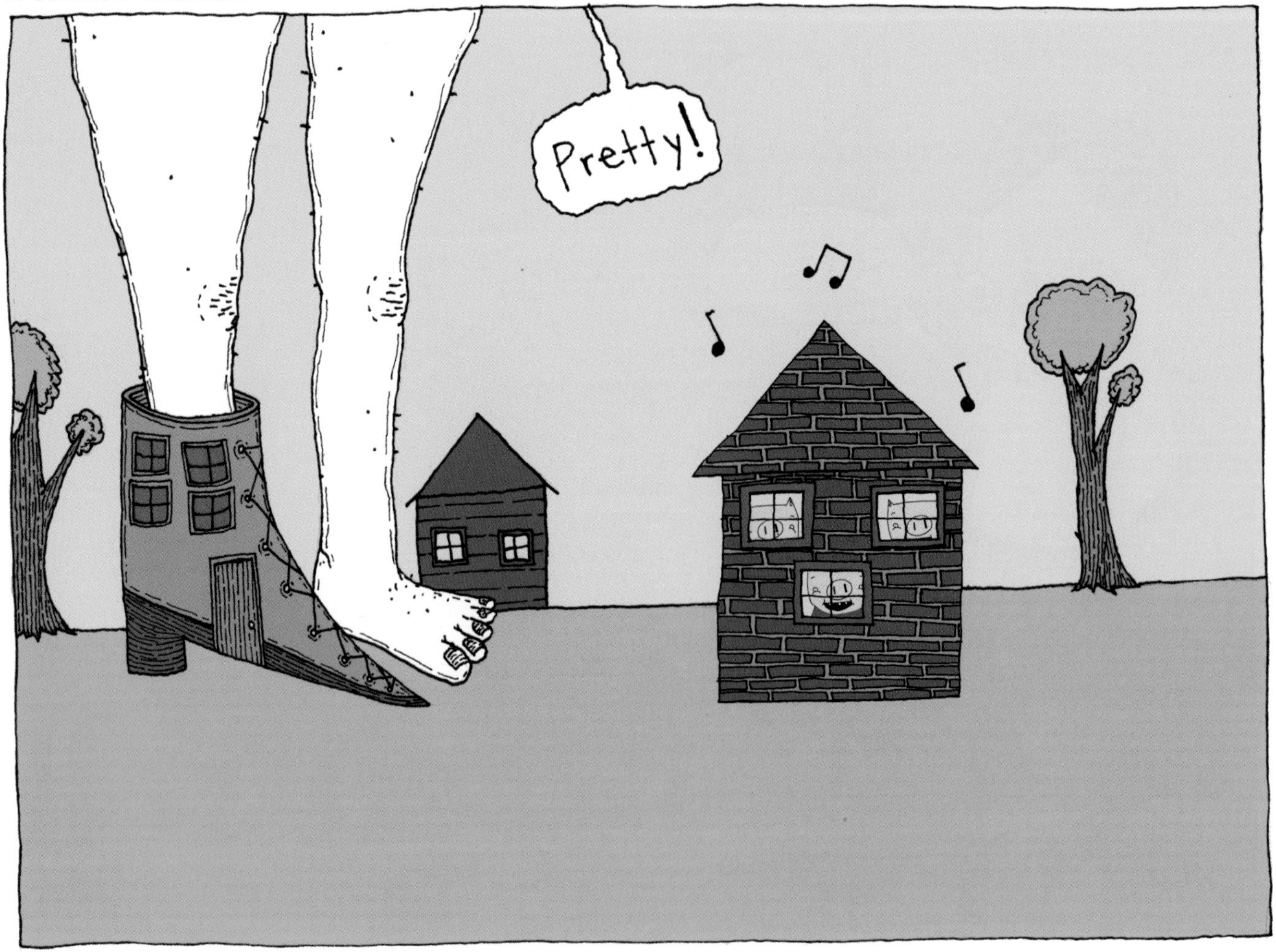
Pretty!

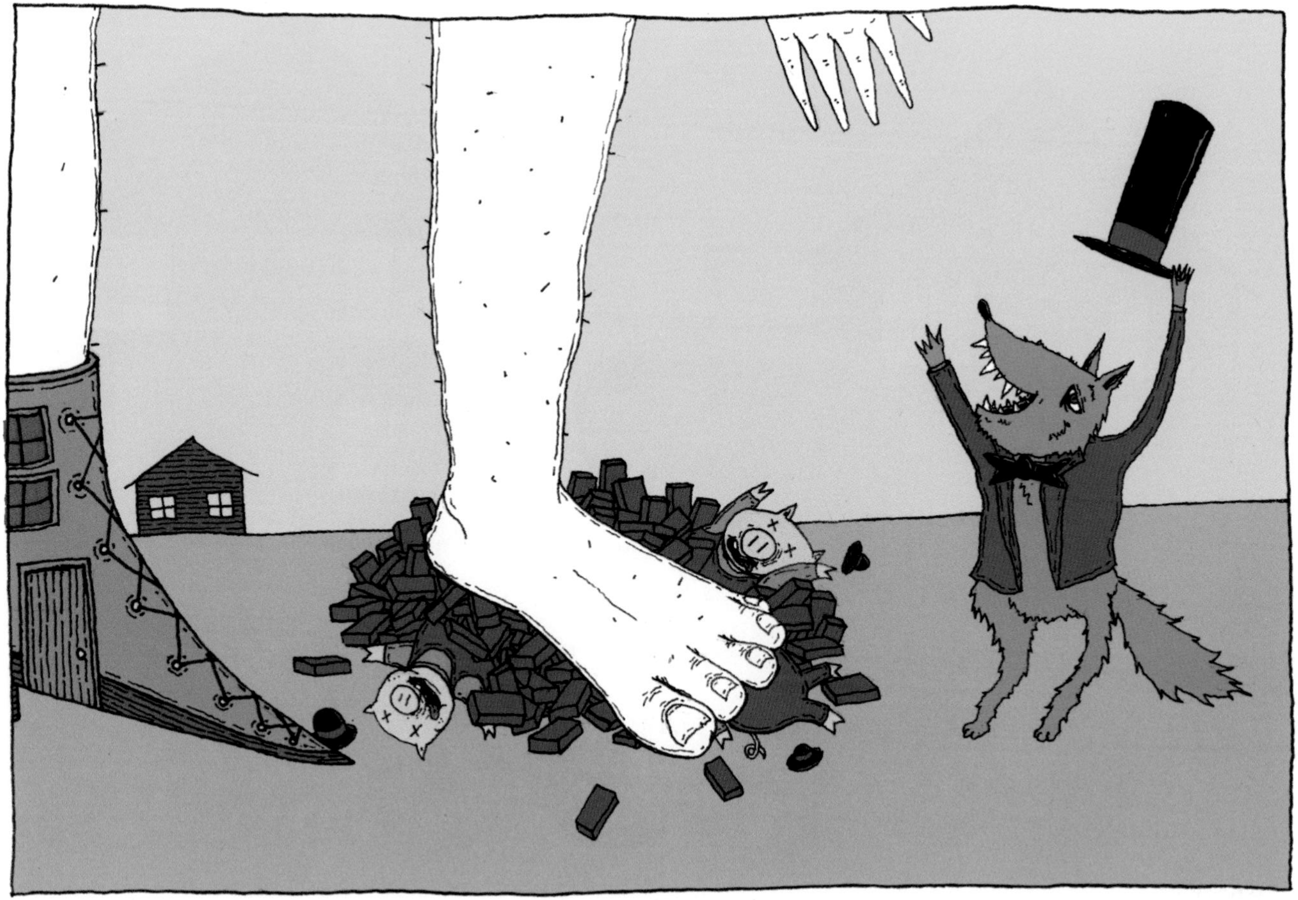

# Rapunzel's Bicycle

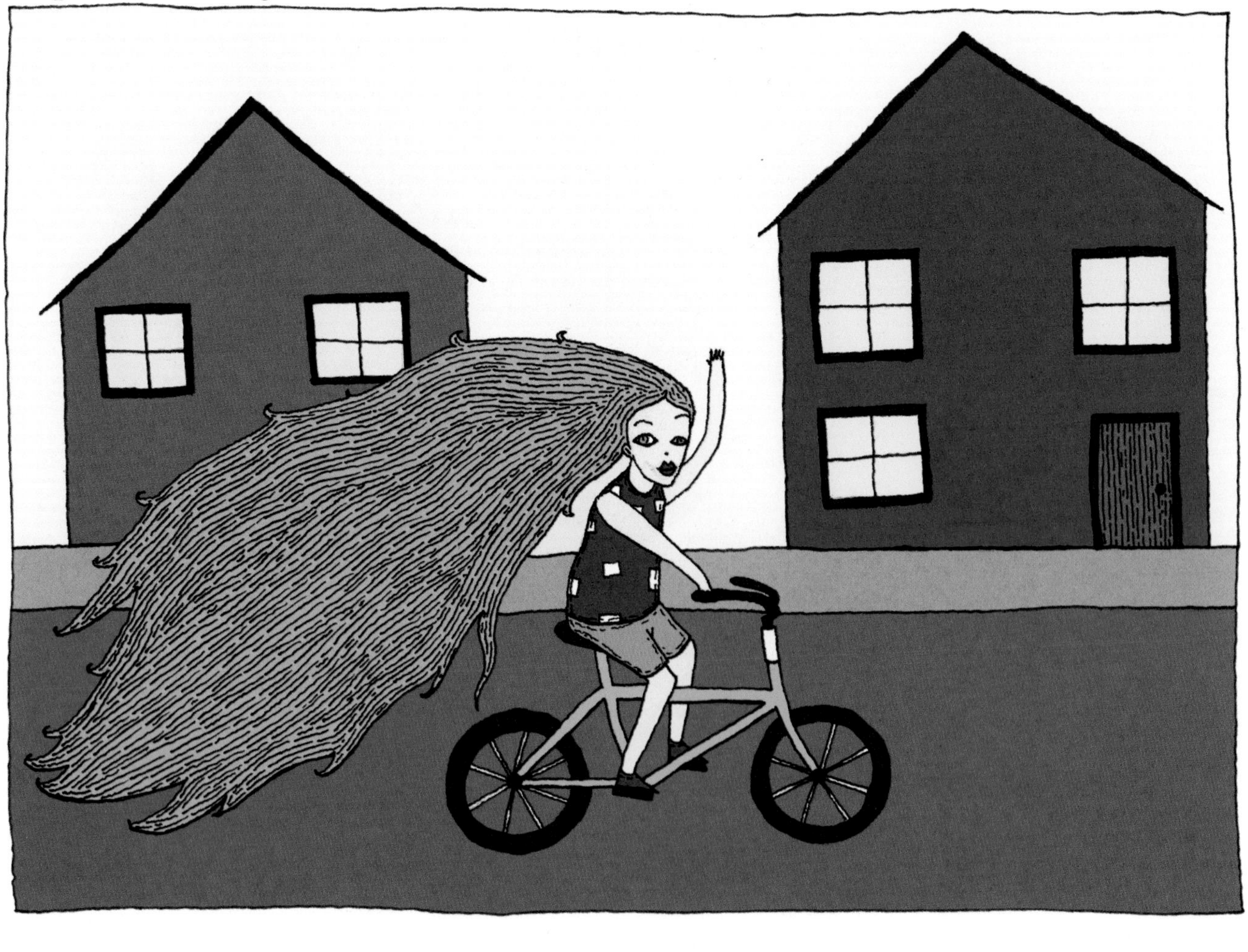

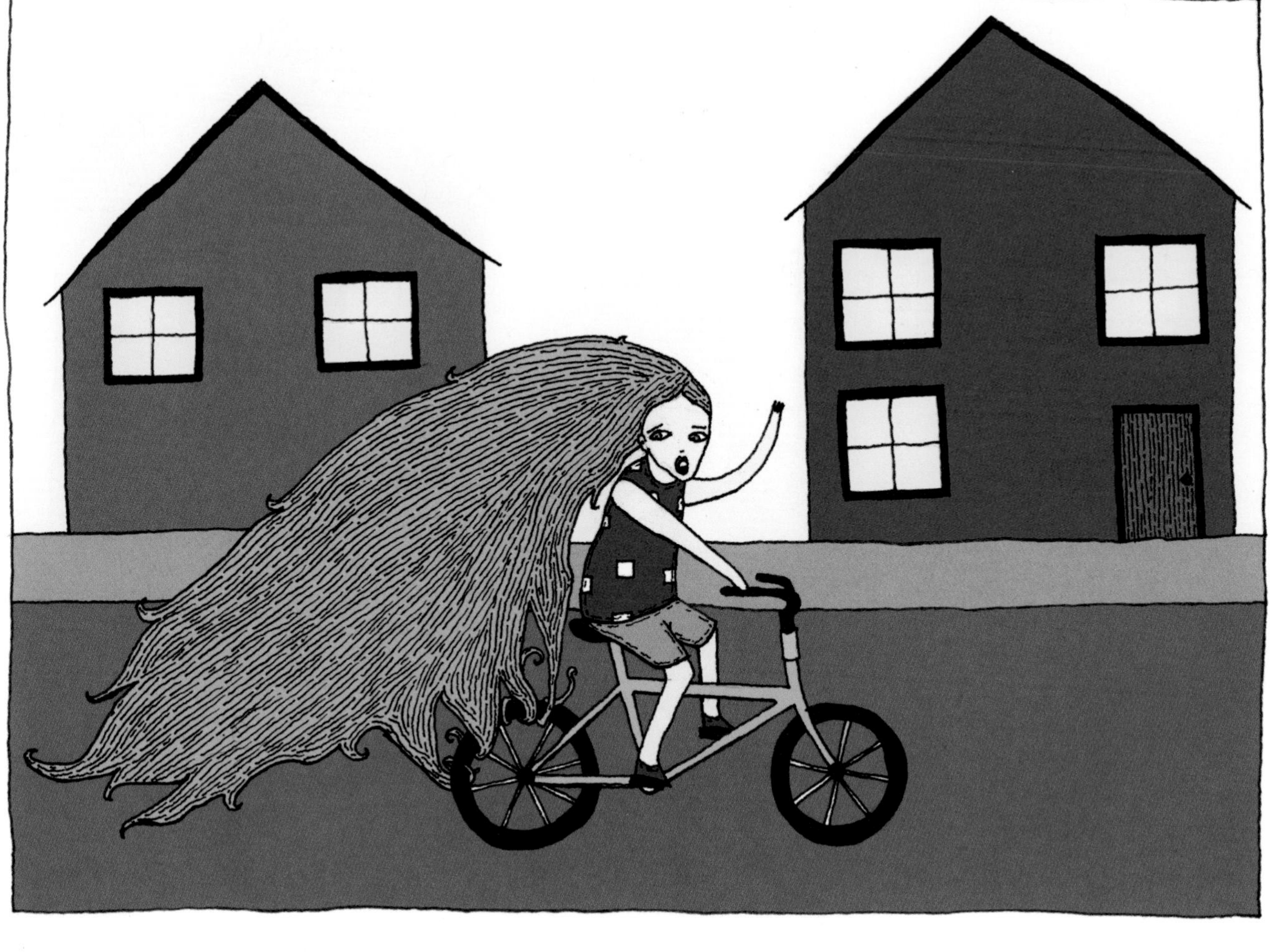

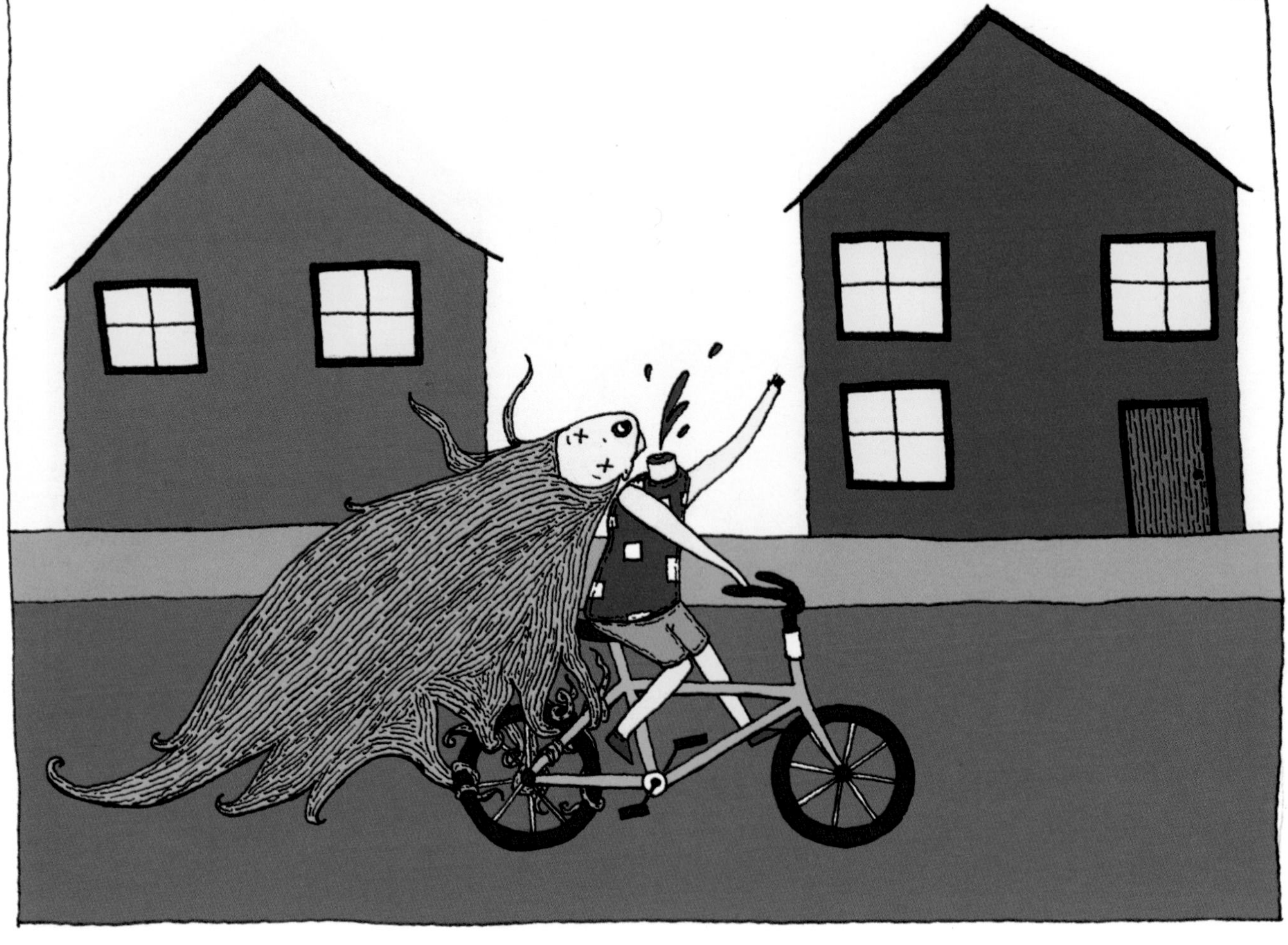

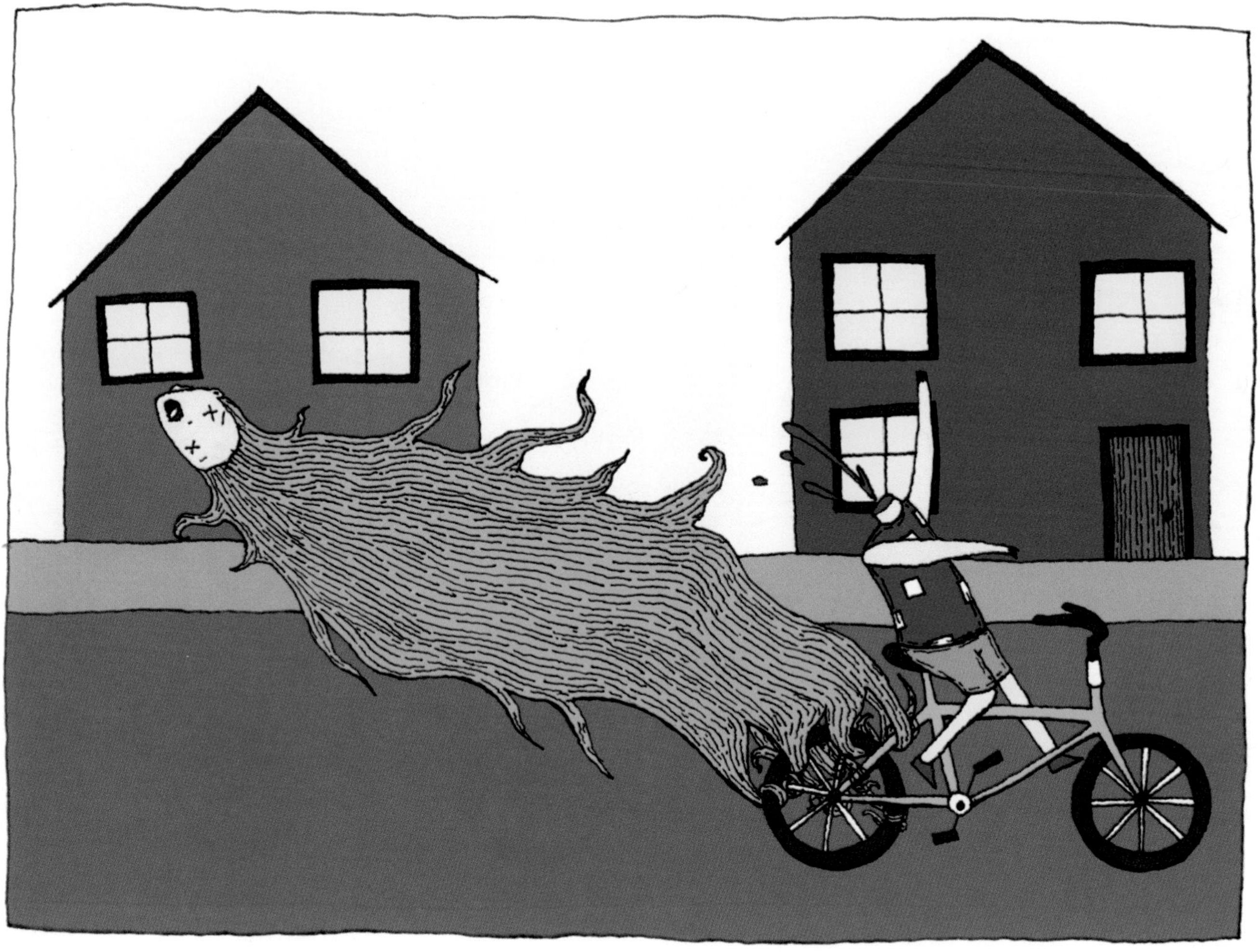

## Goldilocks and Three Bears

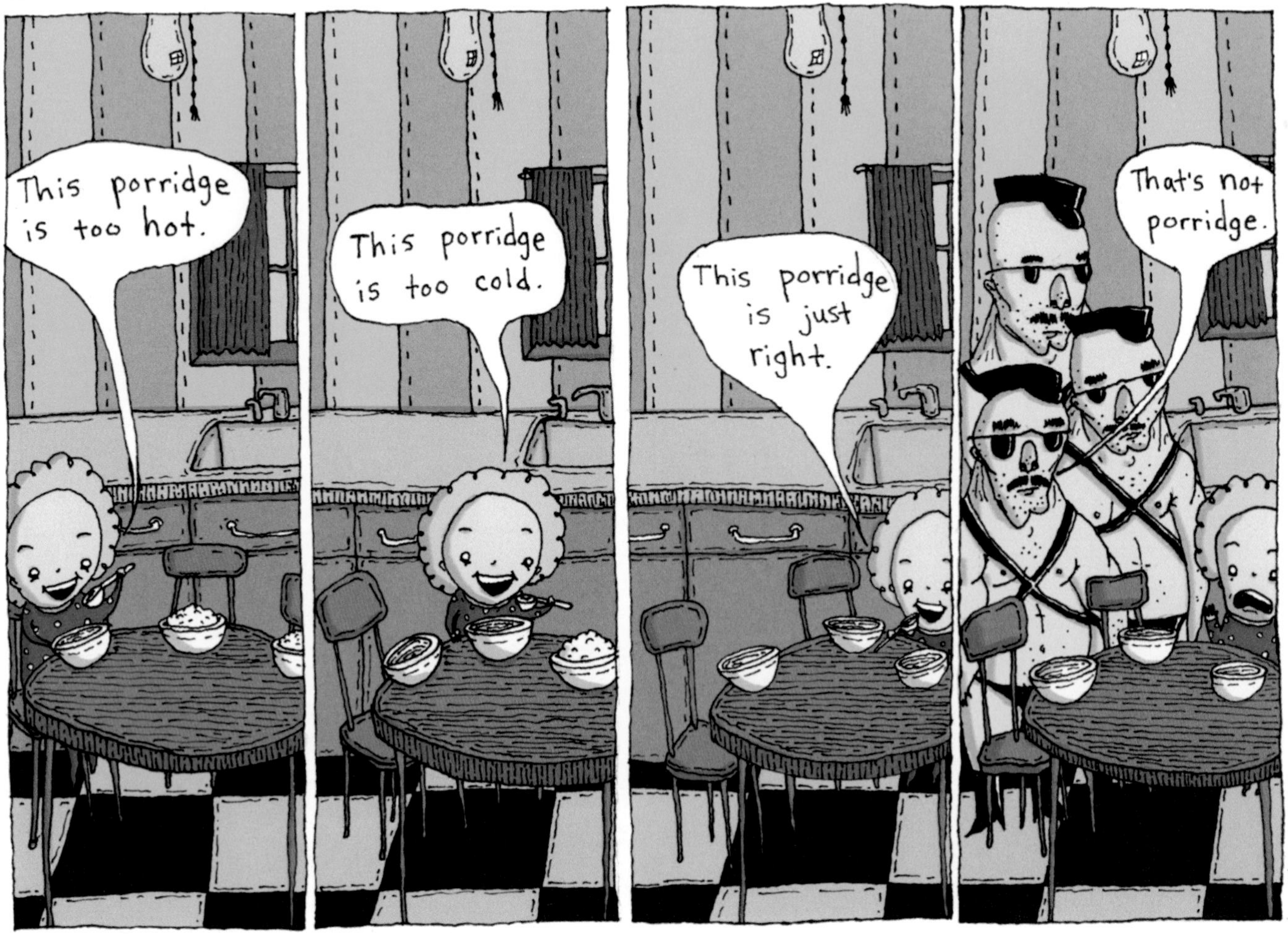
This porridge is too hot.
This porridge is too cold.
This porridge is just right.
That's not porridge.

Tasteful Date

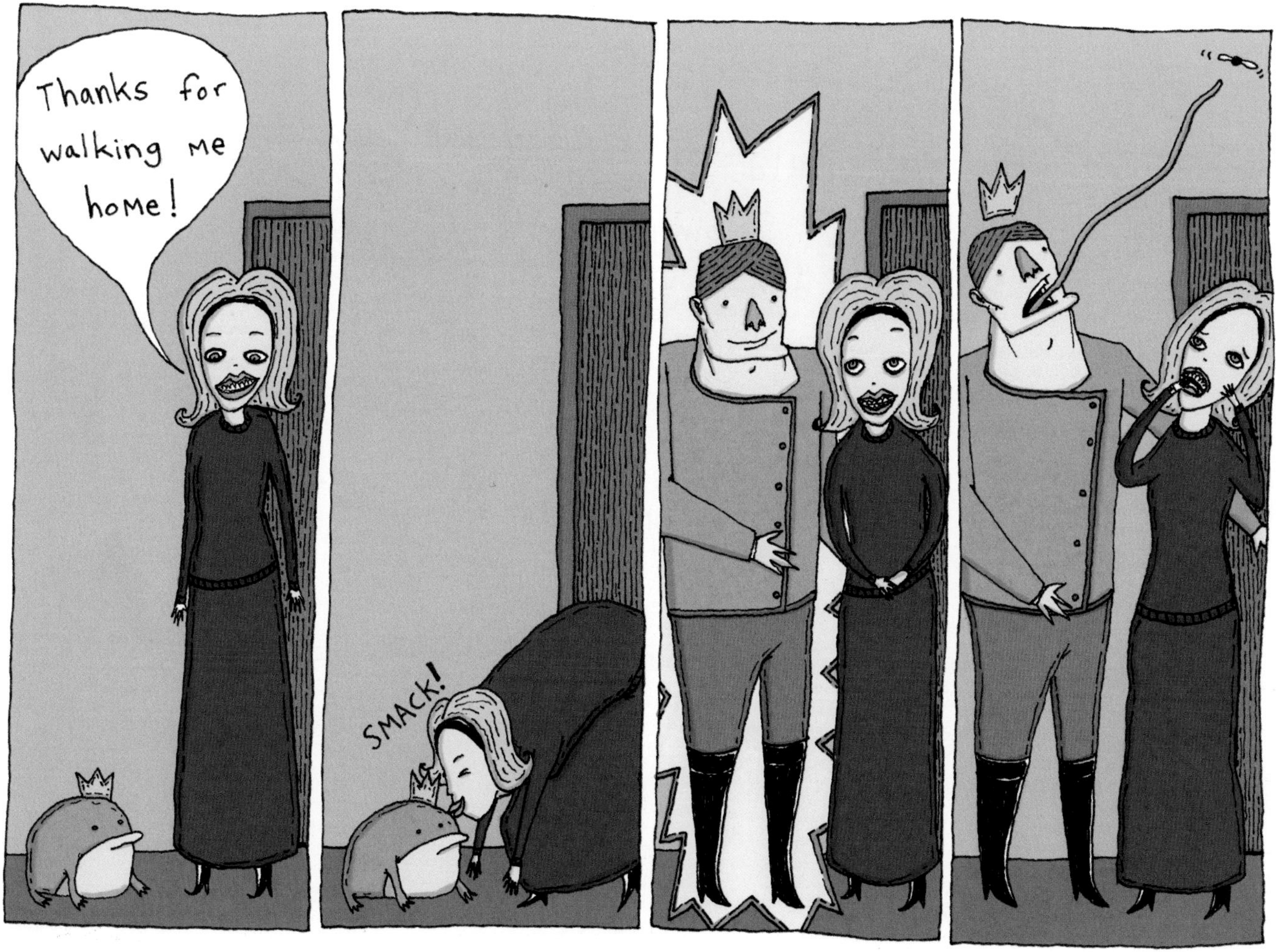
Thanks for walking me home!
SMACK!

Blind Obedience

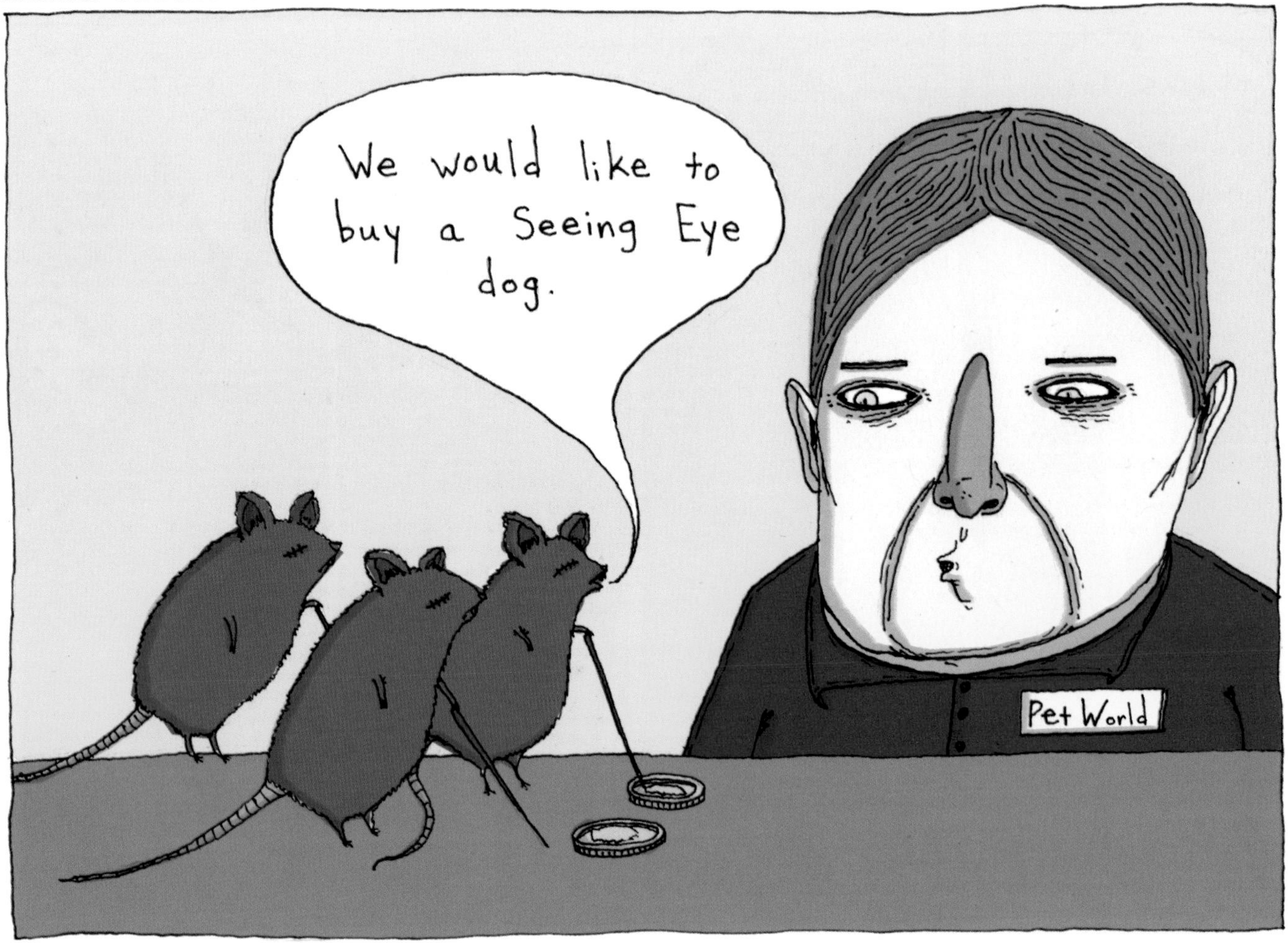
We would like to buy a Seeing Eye dog.
Pet World

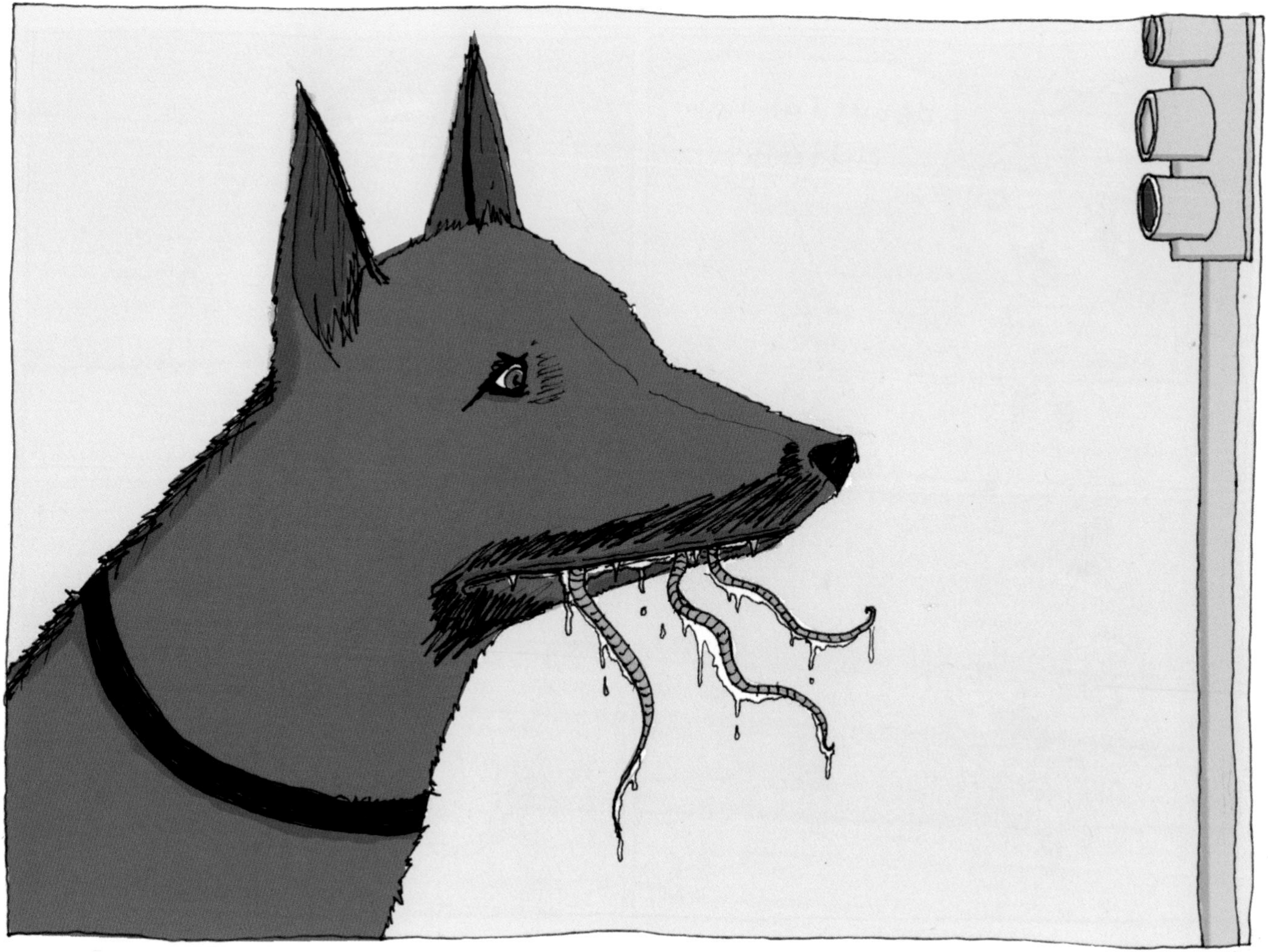

What Really Happened

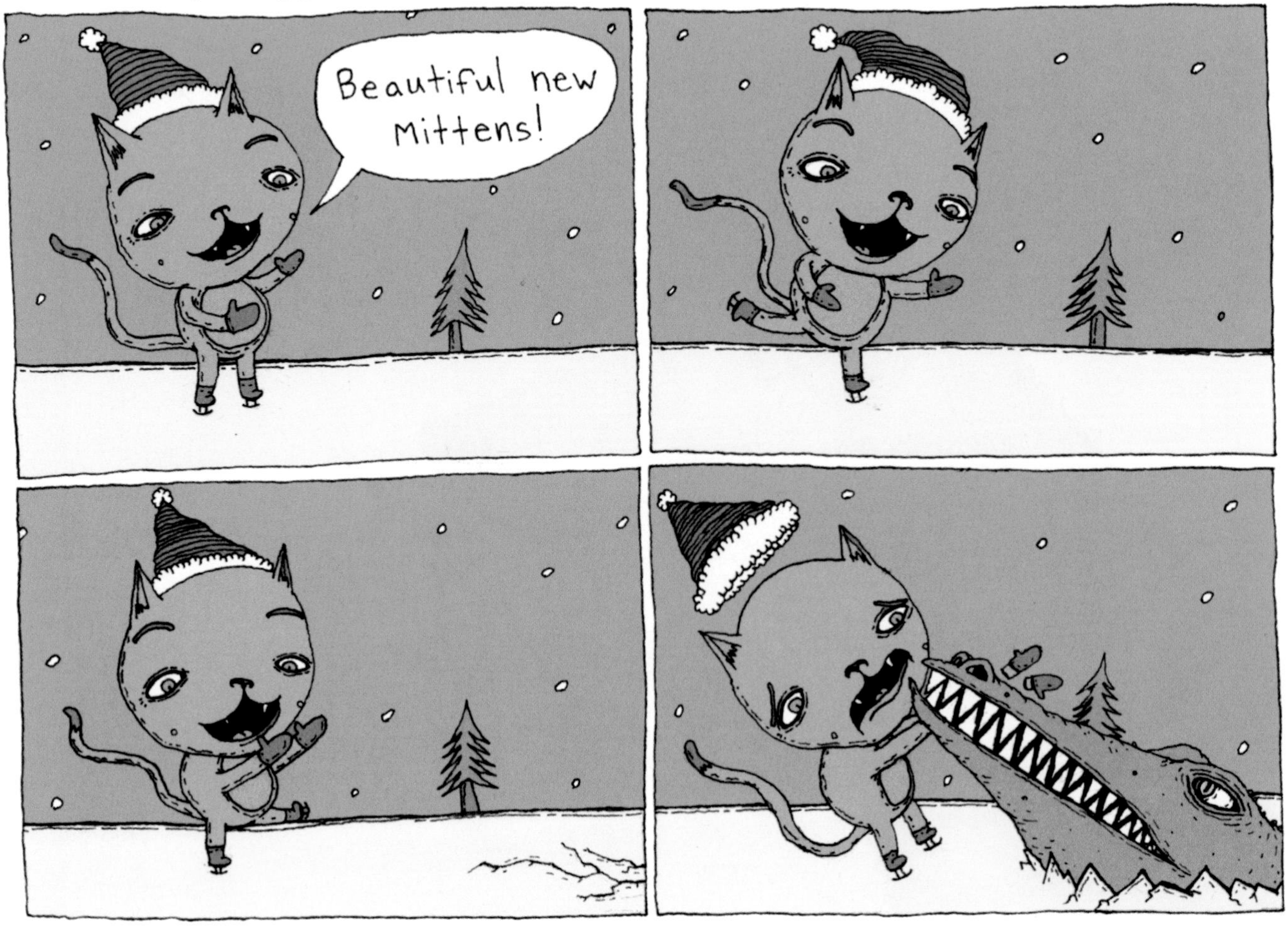
Beautiful new Mittens!

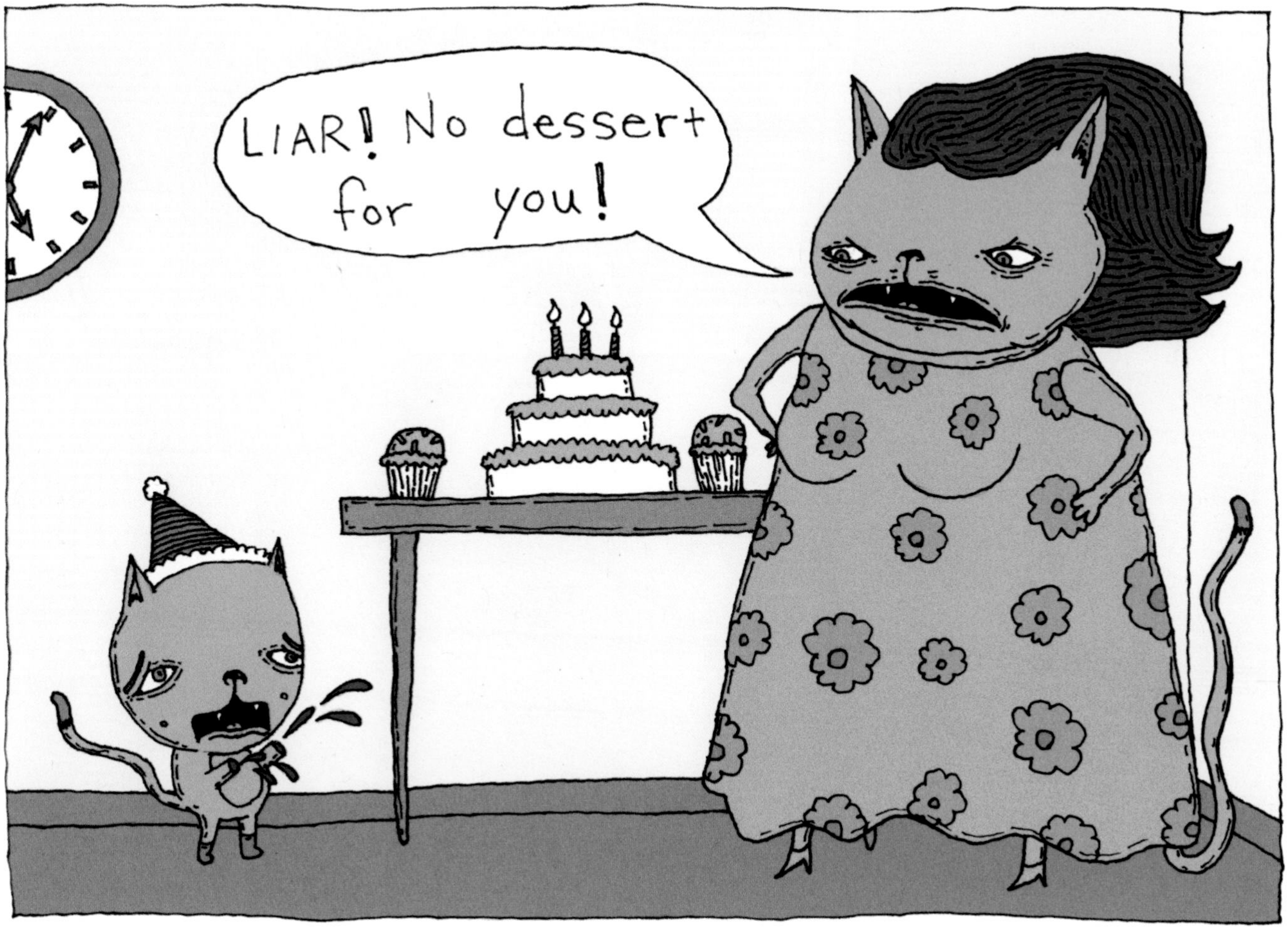
LIAR! No dessert for you!

Rapunzel's Garbage Disposal

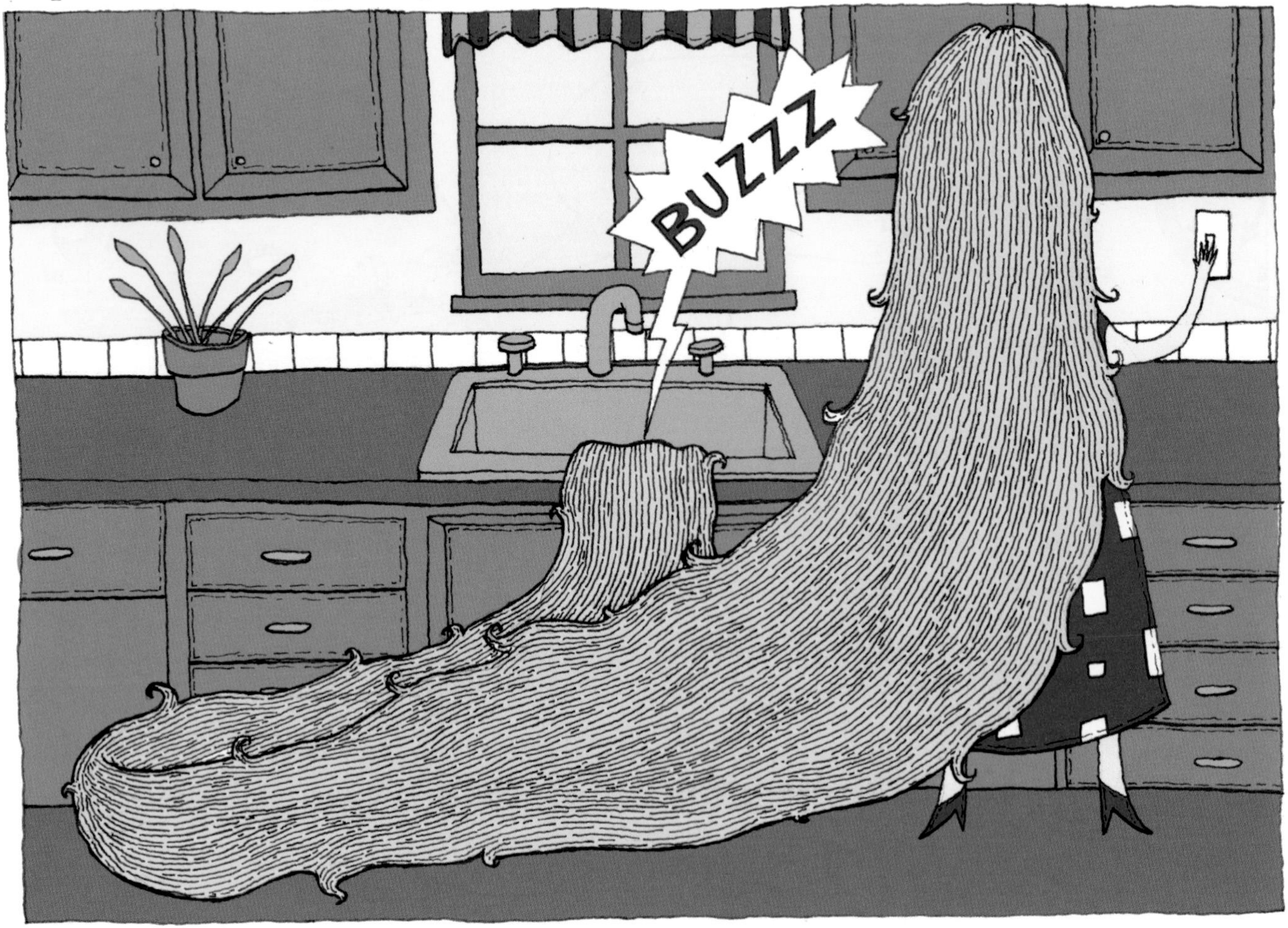
BUZZZ

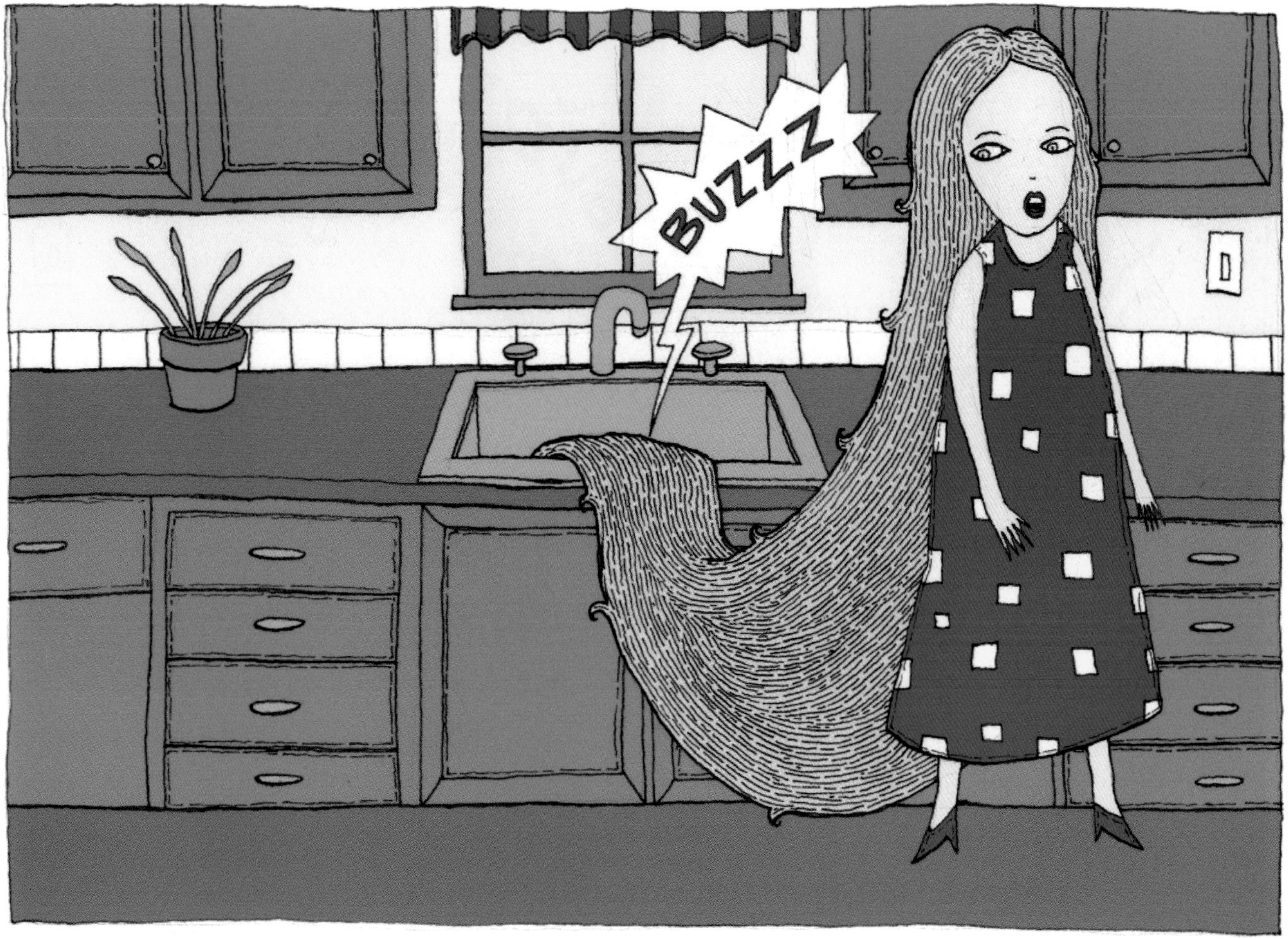
BUZZZ

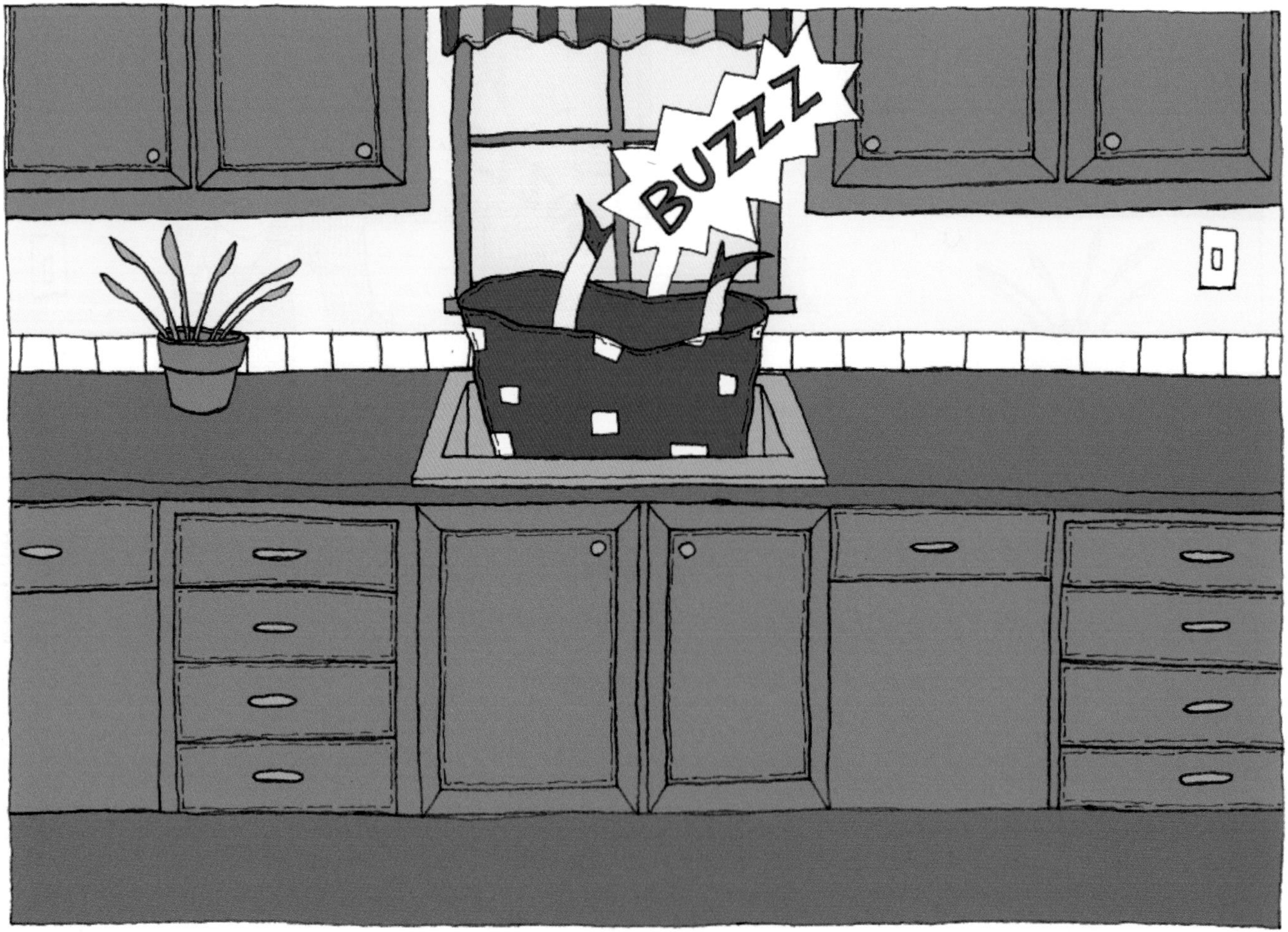
BUZZZ

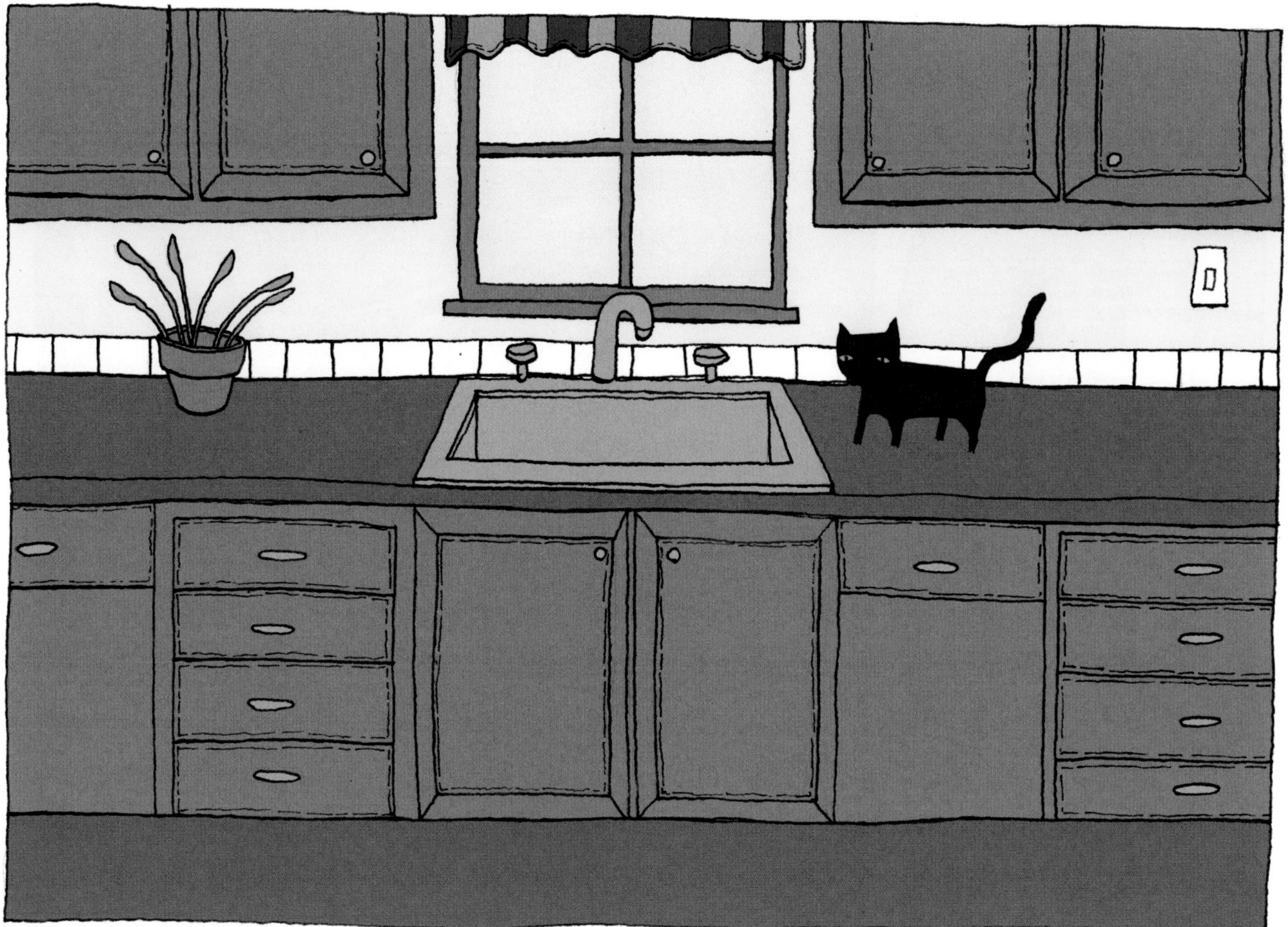

What a Witch

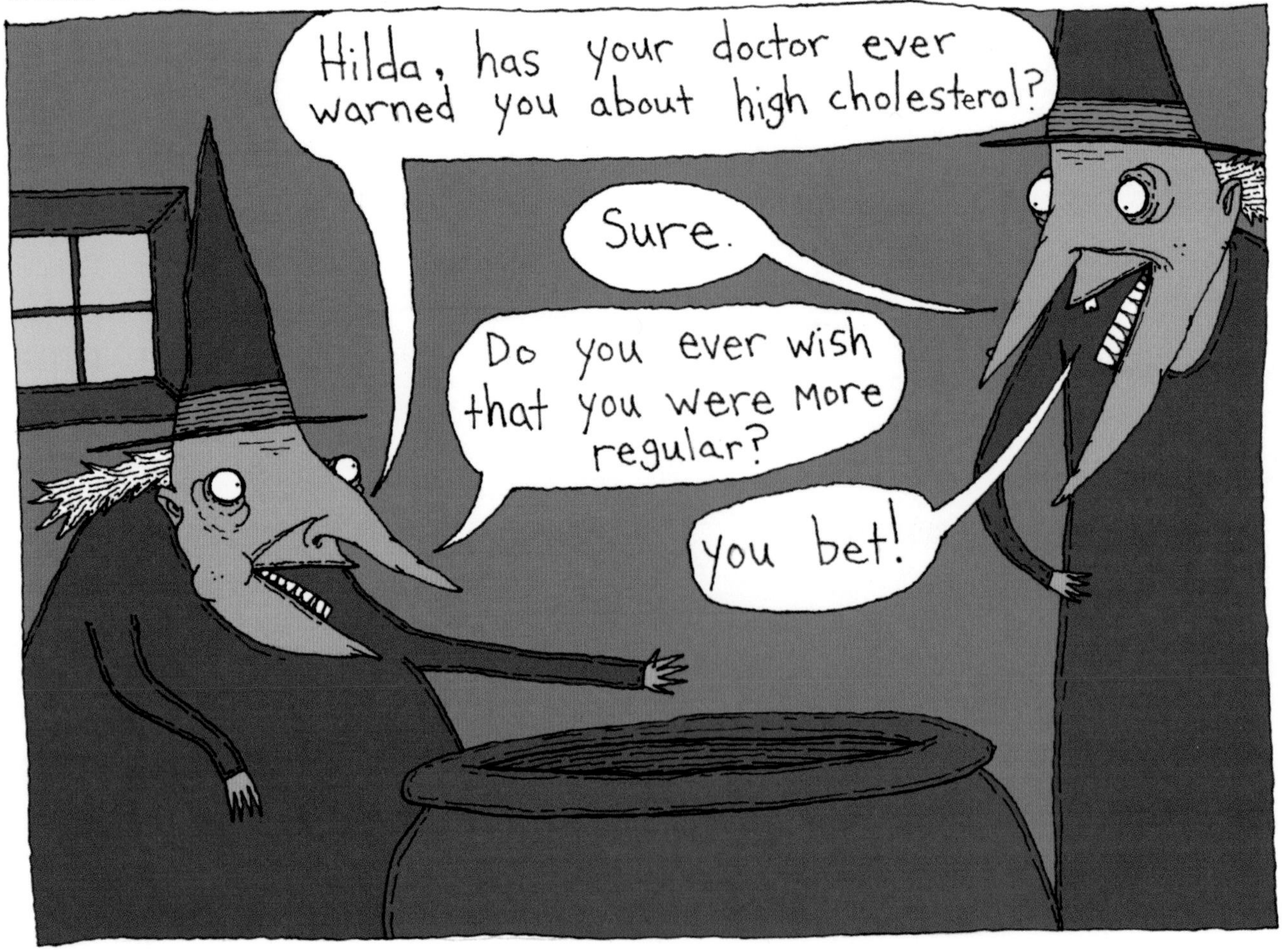
Hilda, has your doctor ever warned you about high cholesterol?
Sure.
Do you ever wish that you were more regular?
You bet!

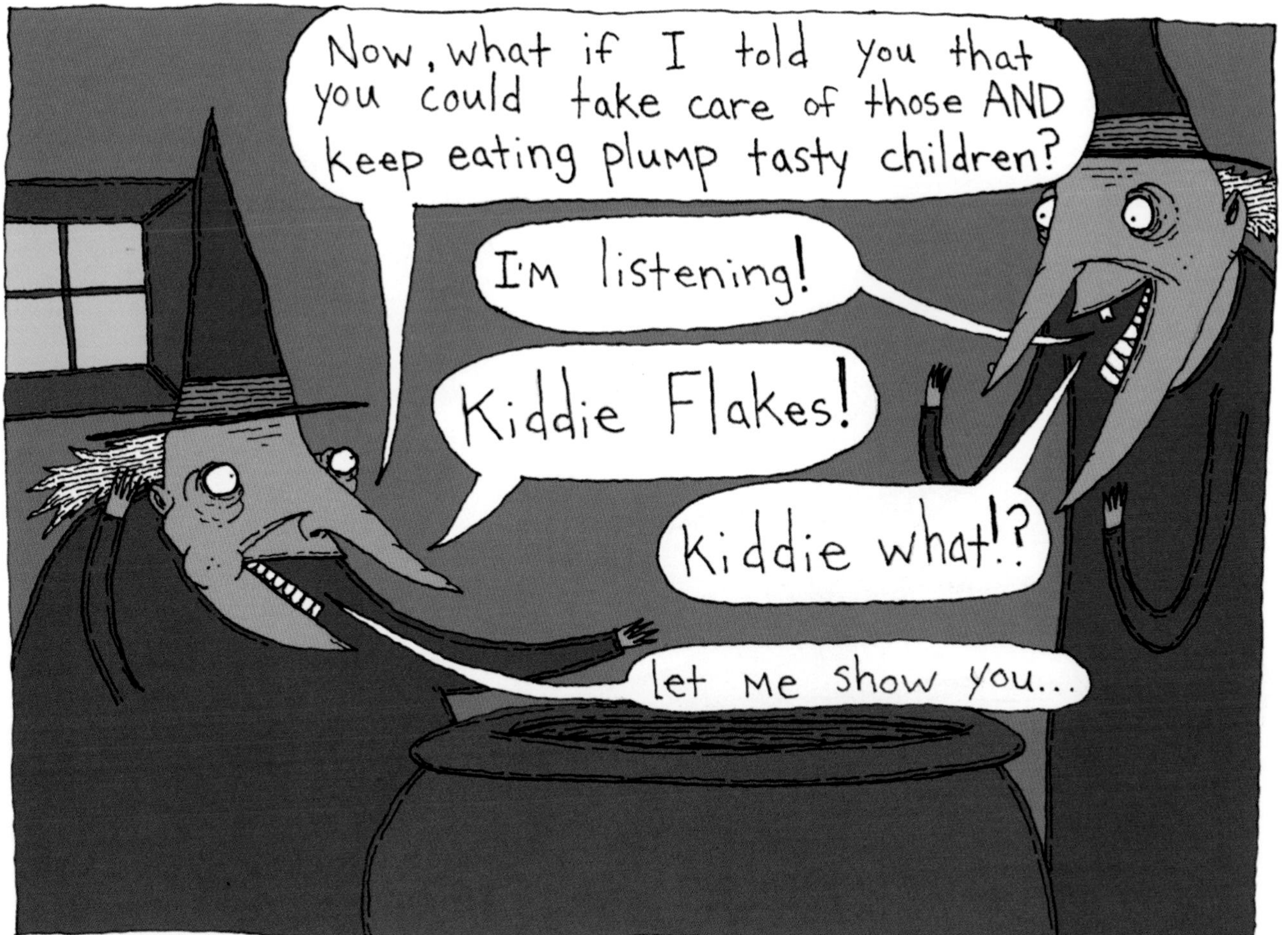
Now, what if I told you that you could take care of those AND keep eating plump tasty children?
I'M listening!
Kiddie Flakes!
Kiddie what!?
let me show you...

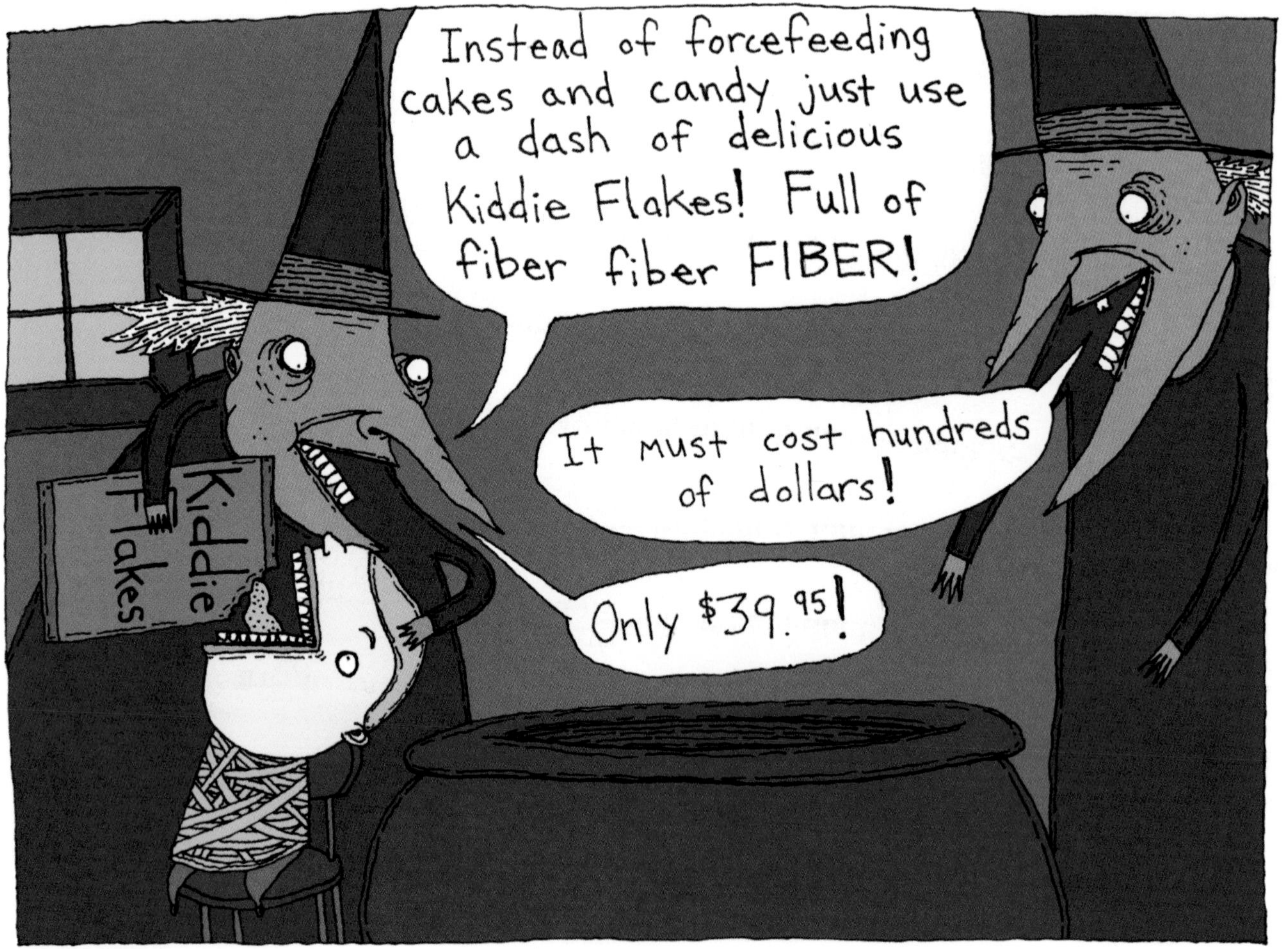
Instead of forcefeeding cakes and candy just use a dash of delicious Kiddie Flakes! Full of fiber fiber FIBER!
It must cost hundreds of dollars!
Only $39.95!
Kiddie Flakes

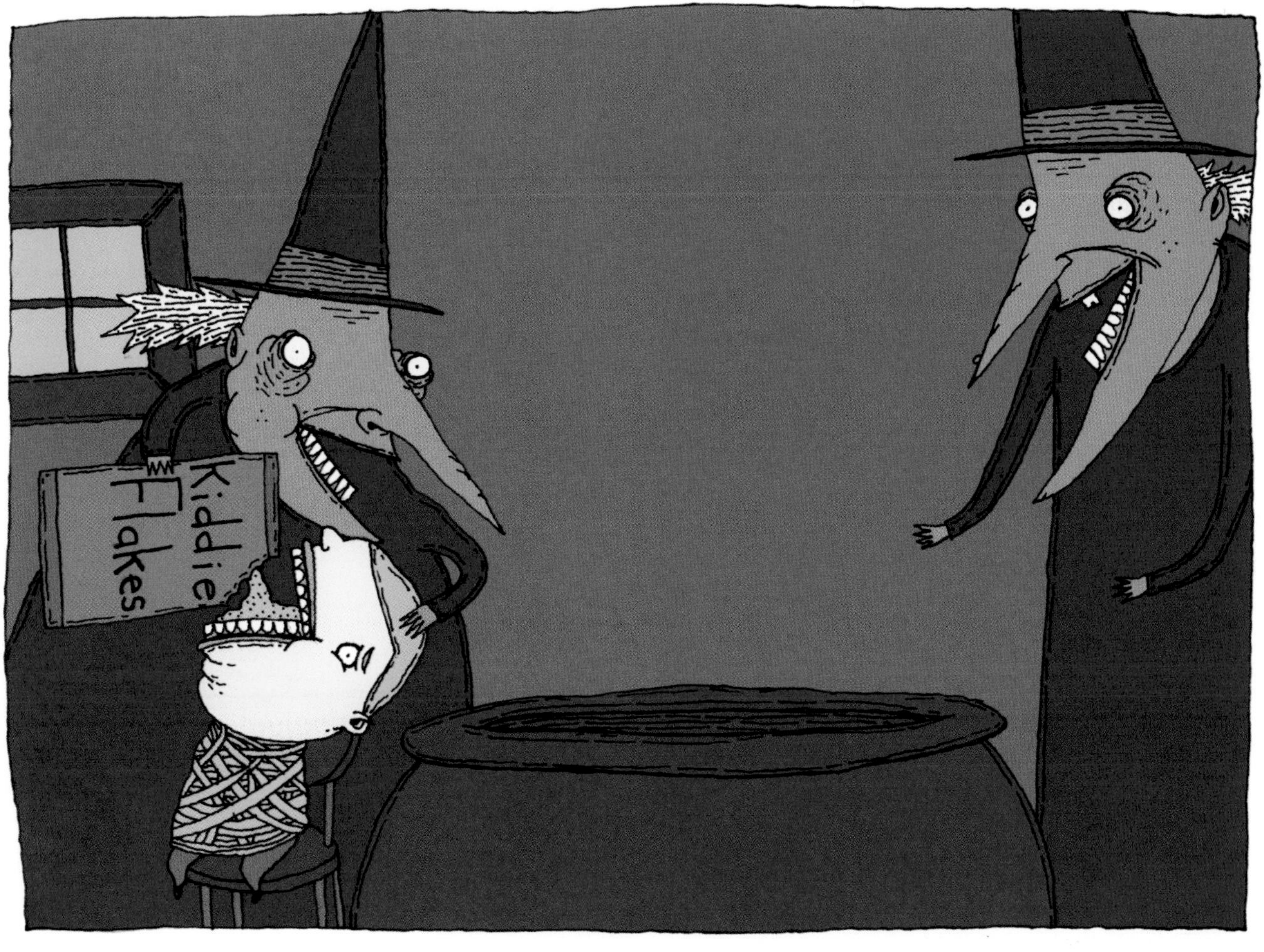
Kiddie Flakes

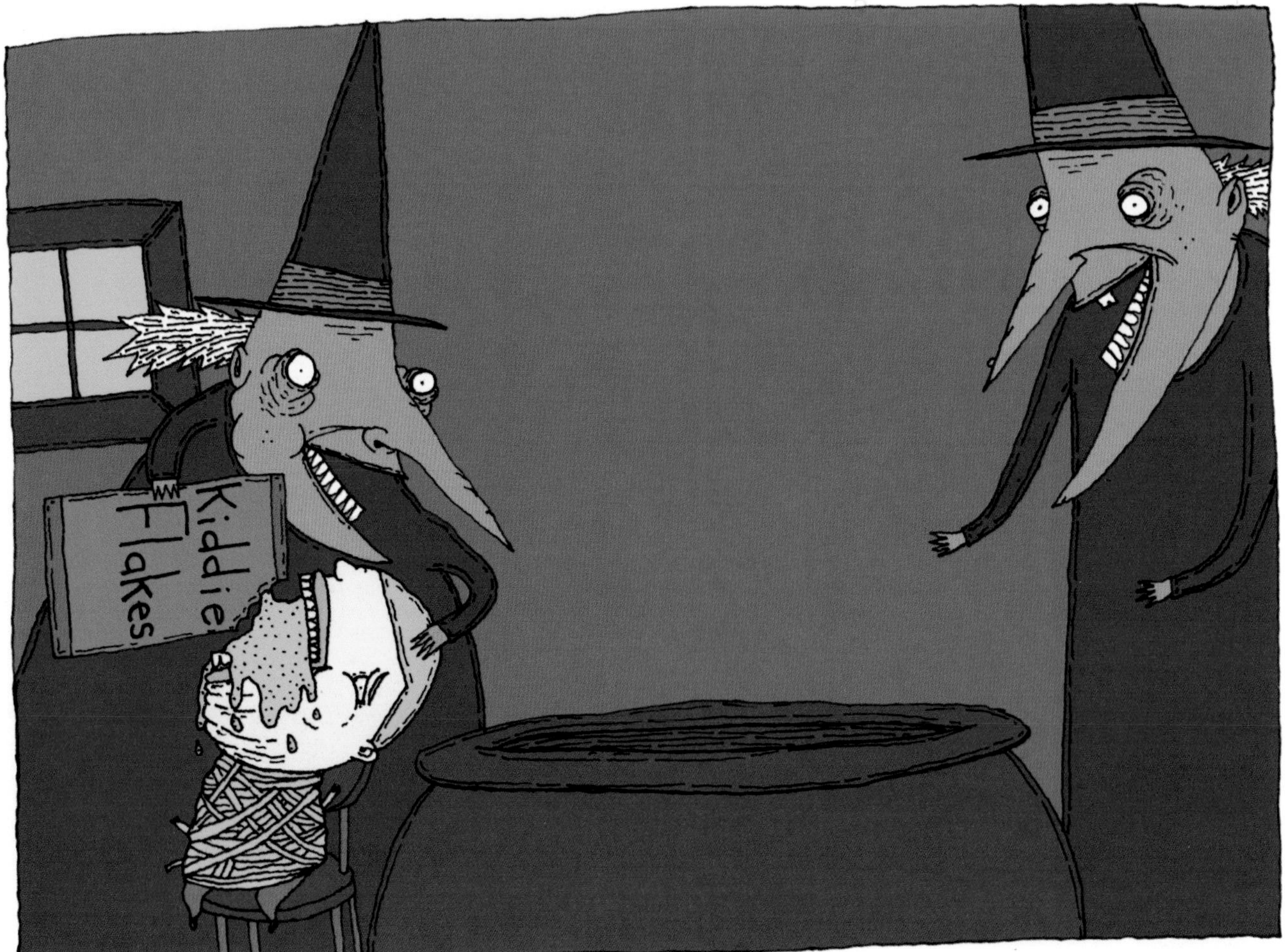
Kiddie Flakes

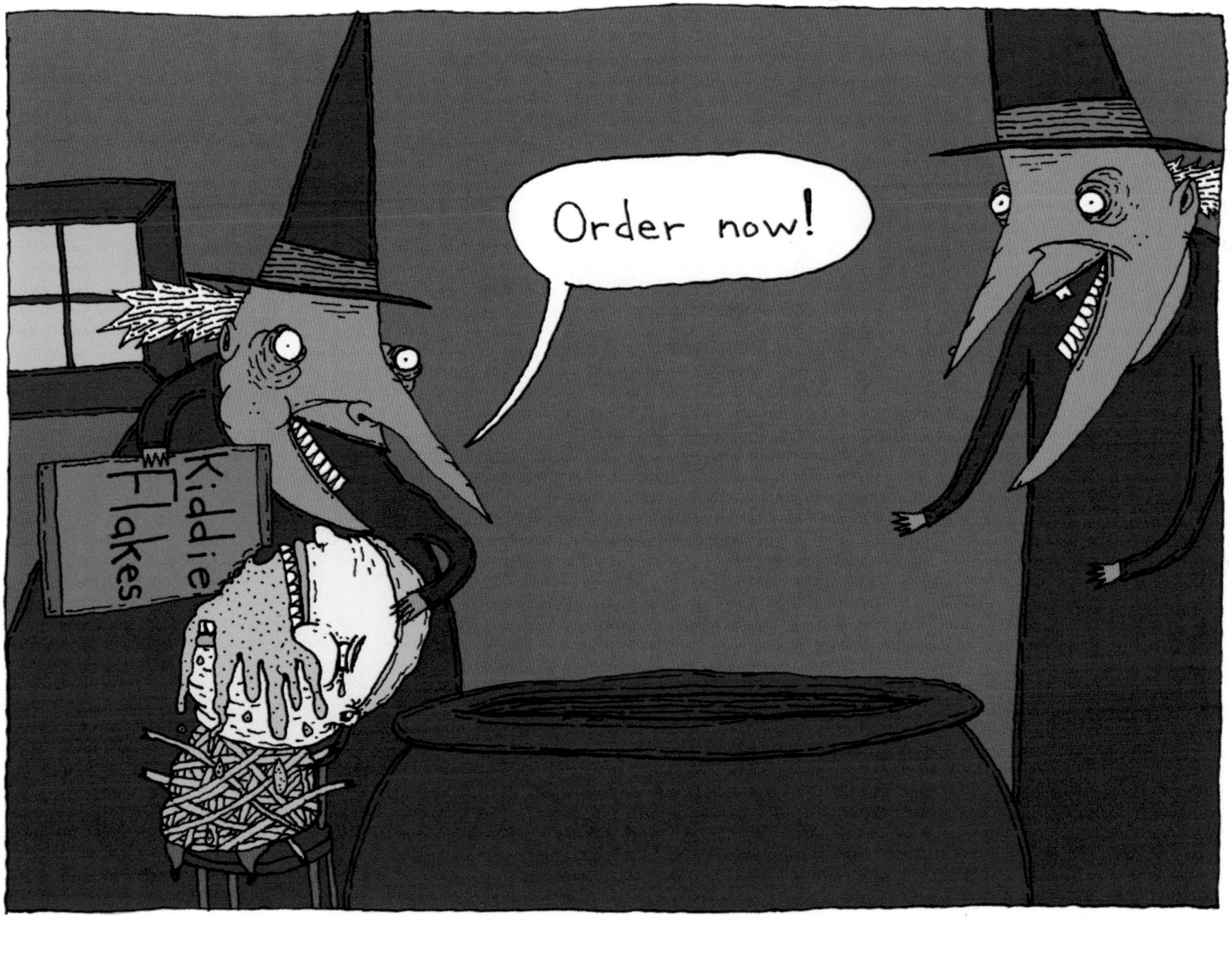
Order now!
Kiddie Flakes

Tortoise and Ladies

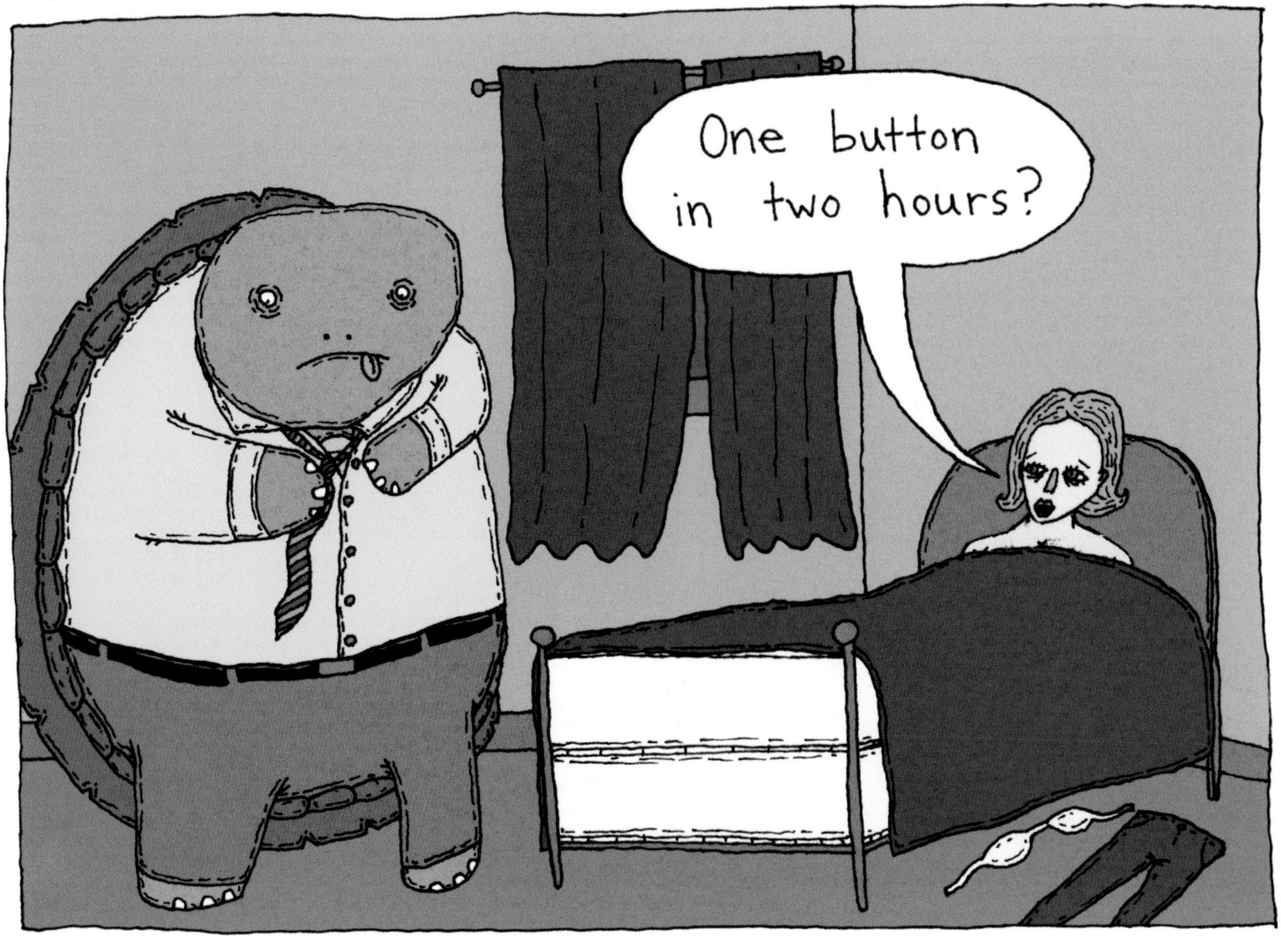
One button in two hours?

Hare and Ladies

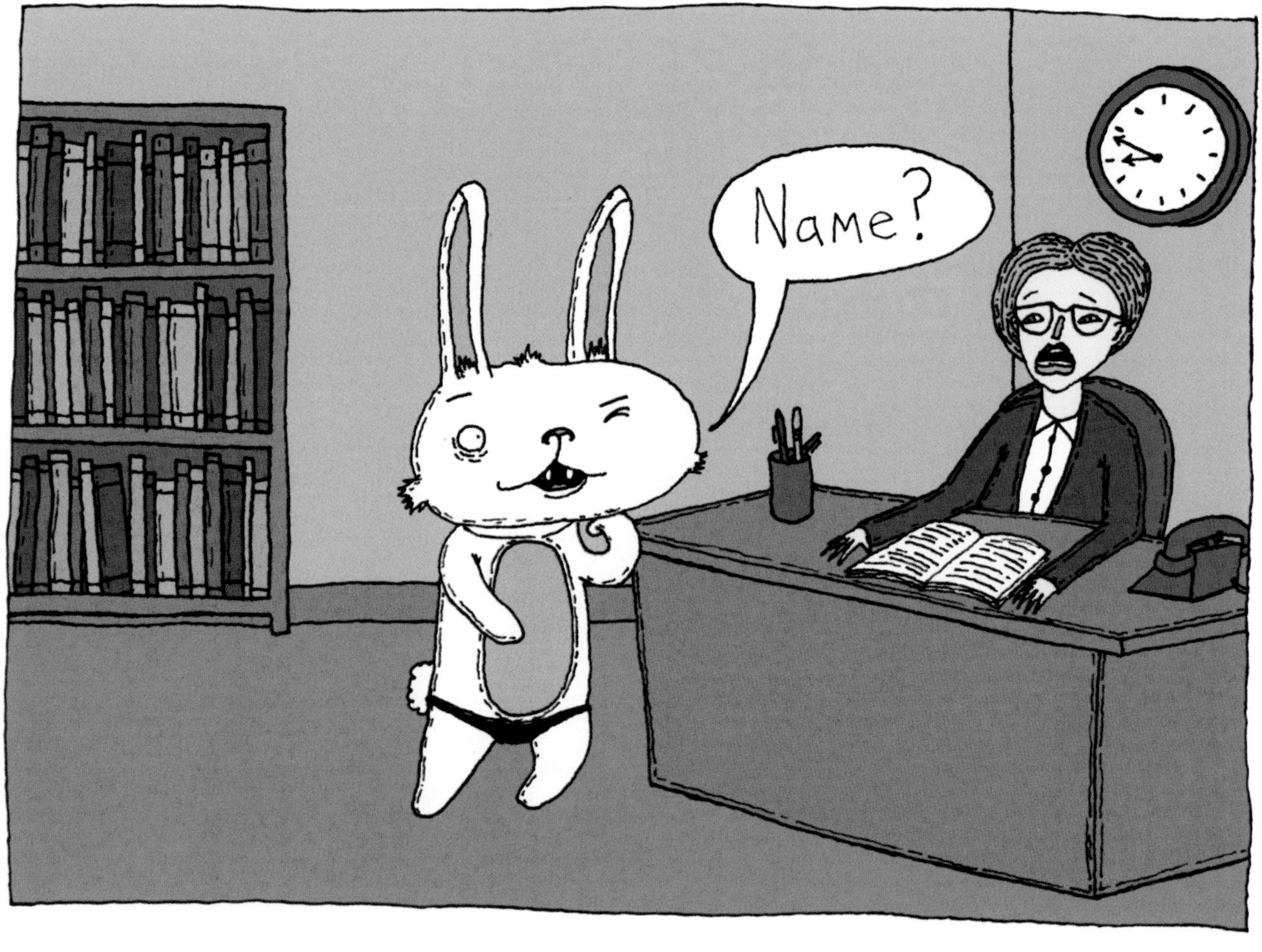
Name?

Tortoise in Surgery

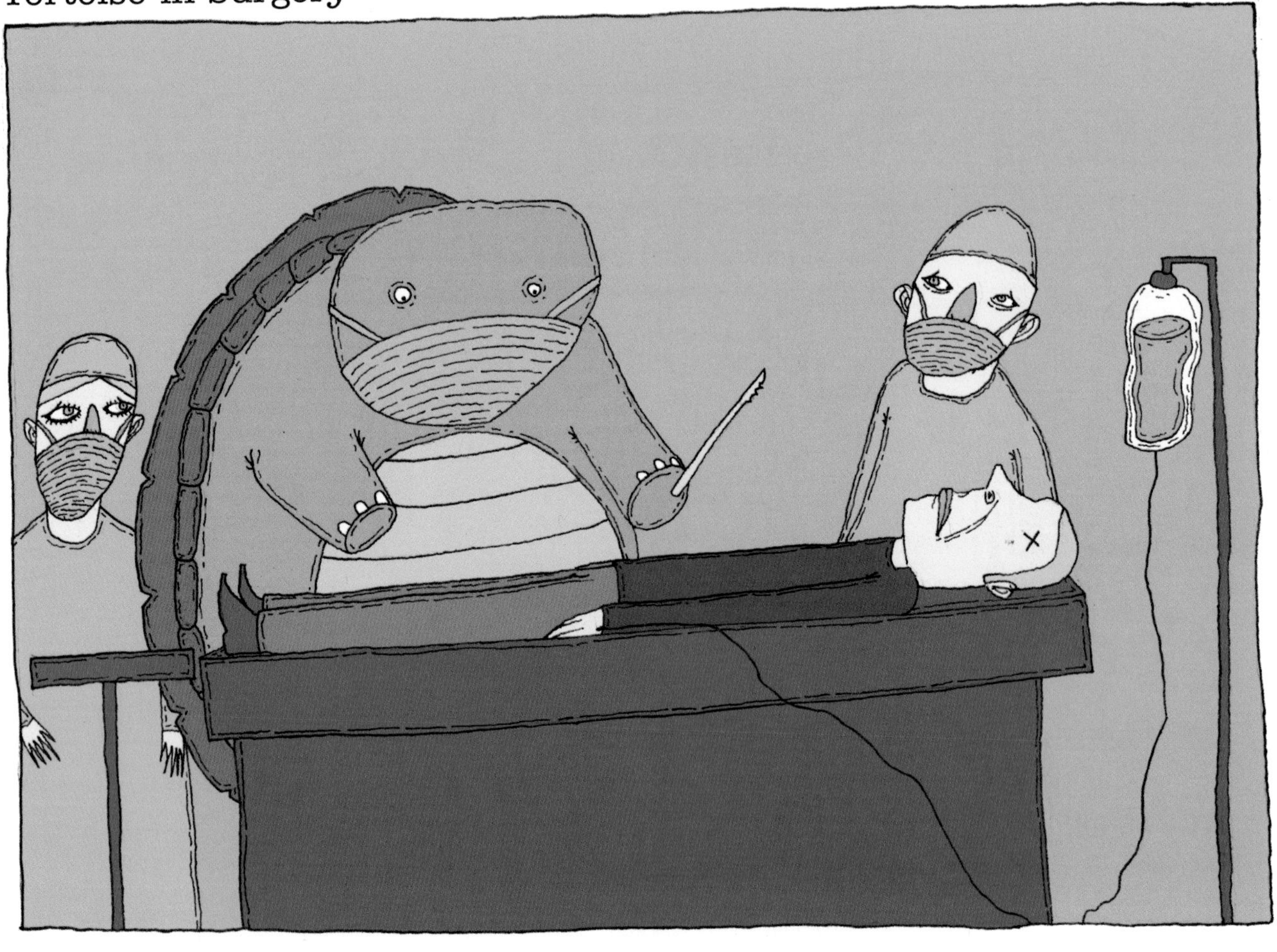

# Hare in Surgery

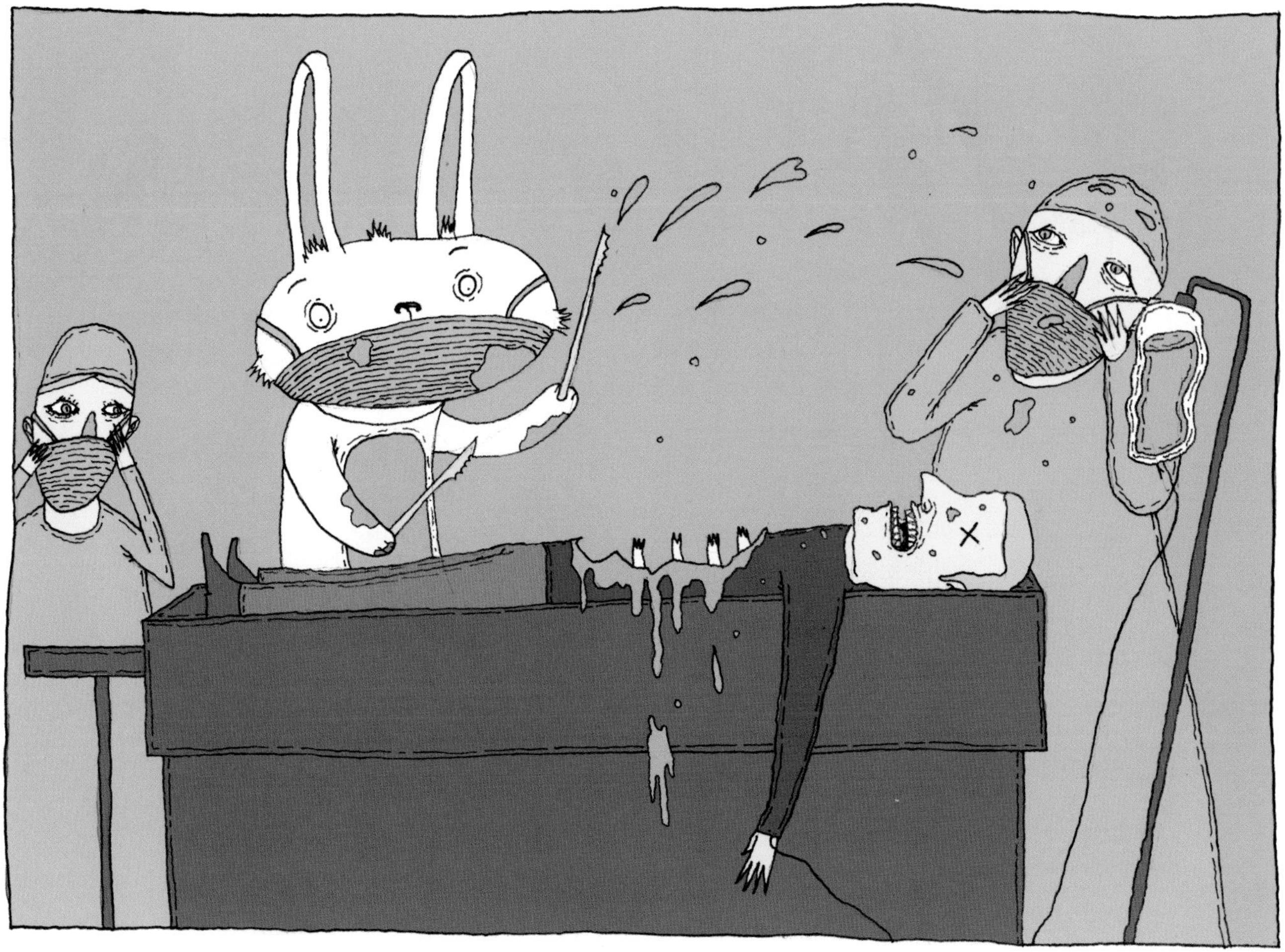

Rapunzel's Cat

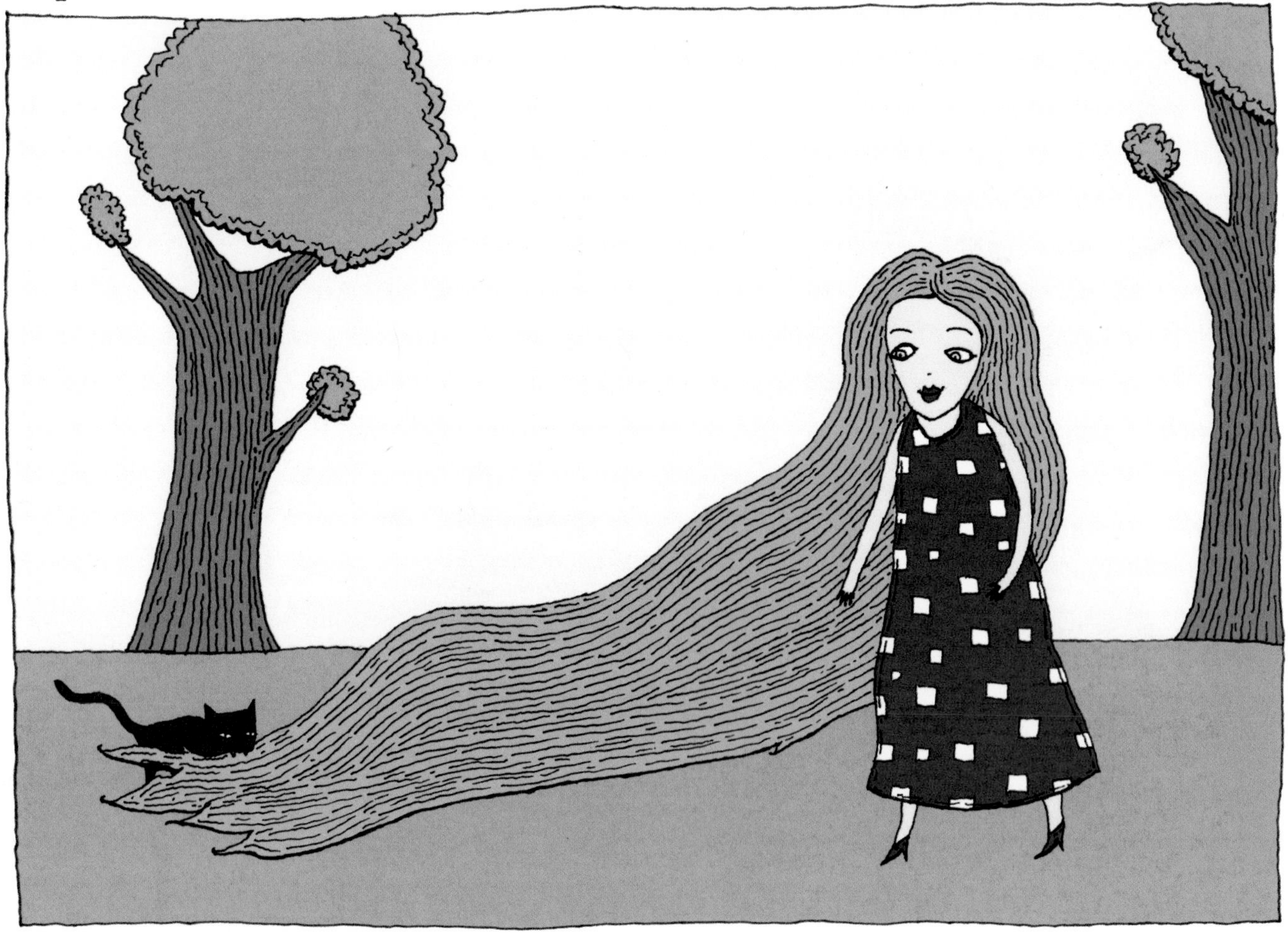

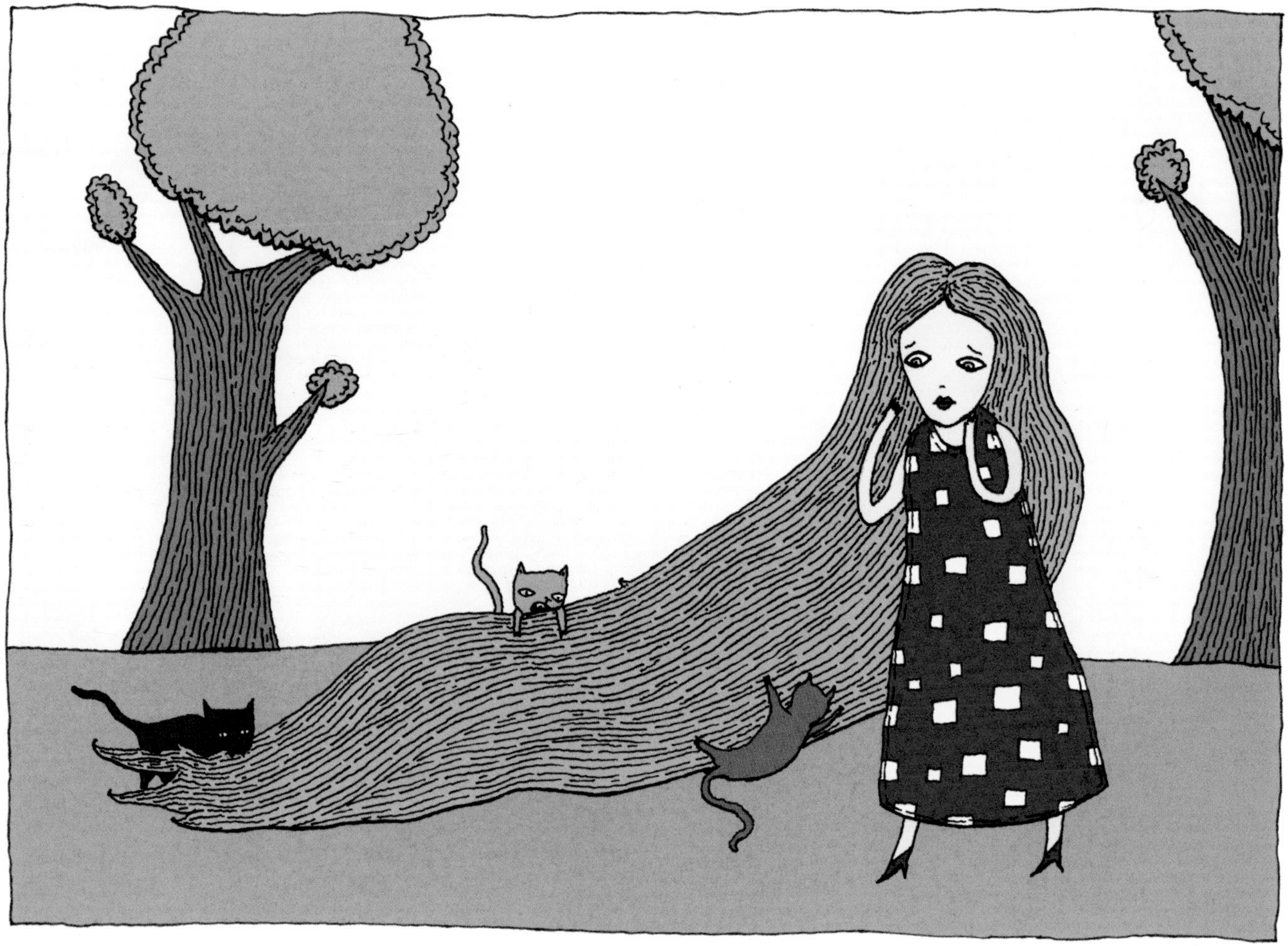

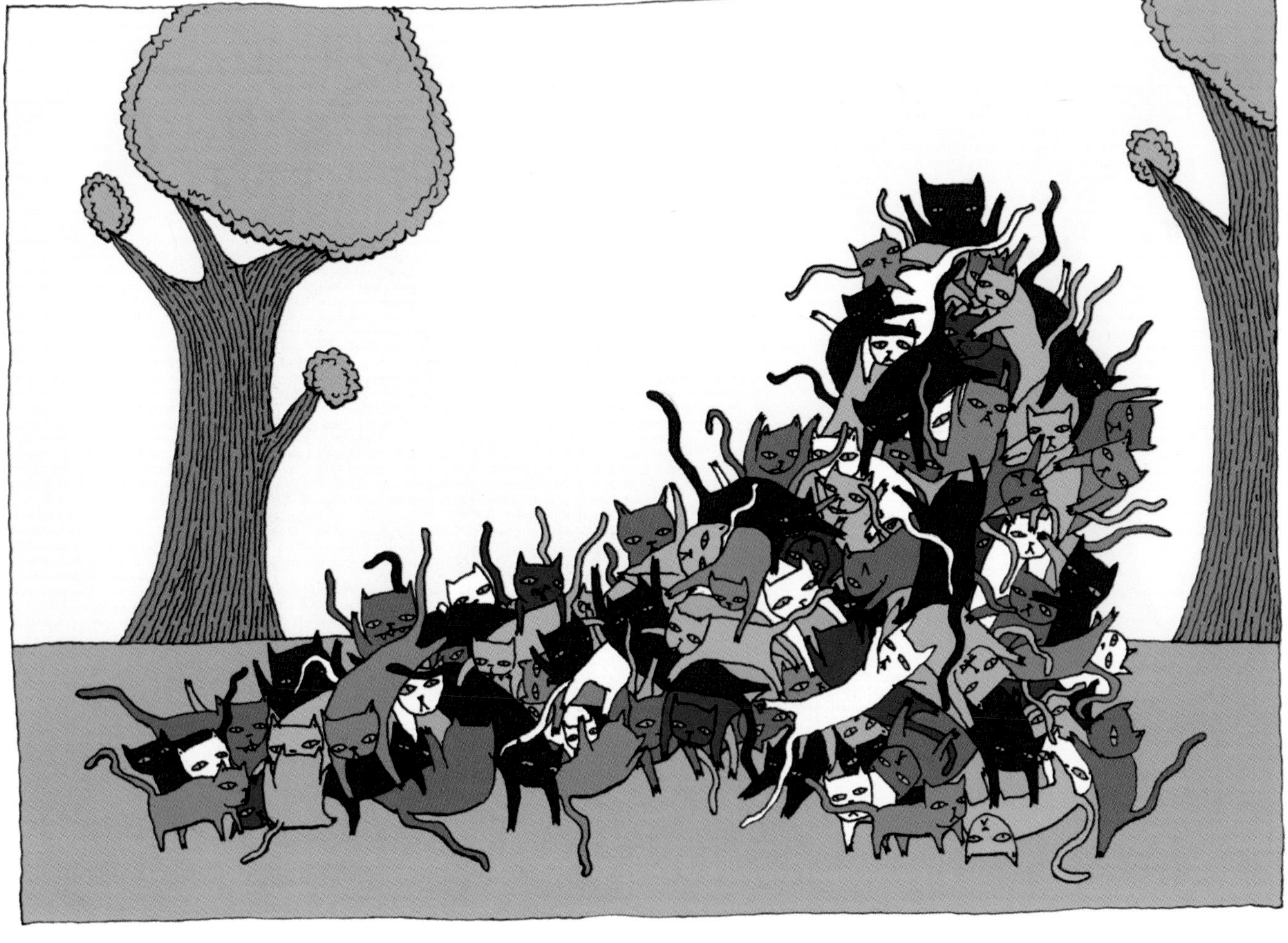

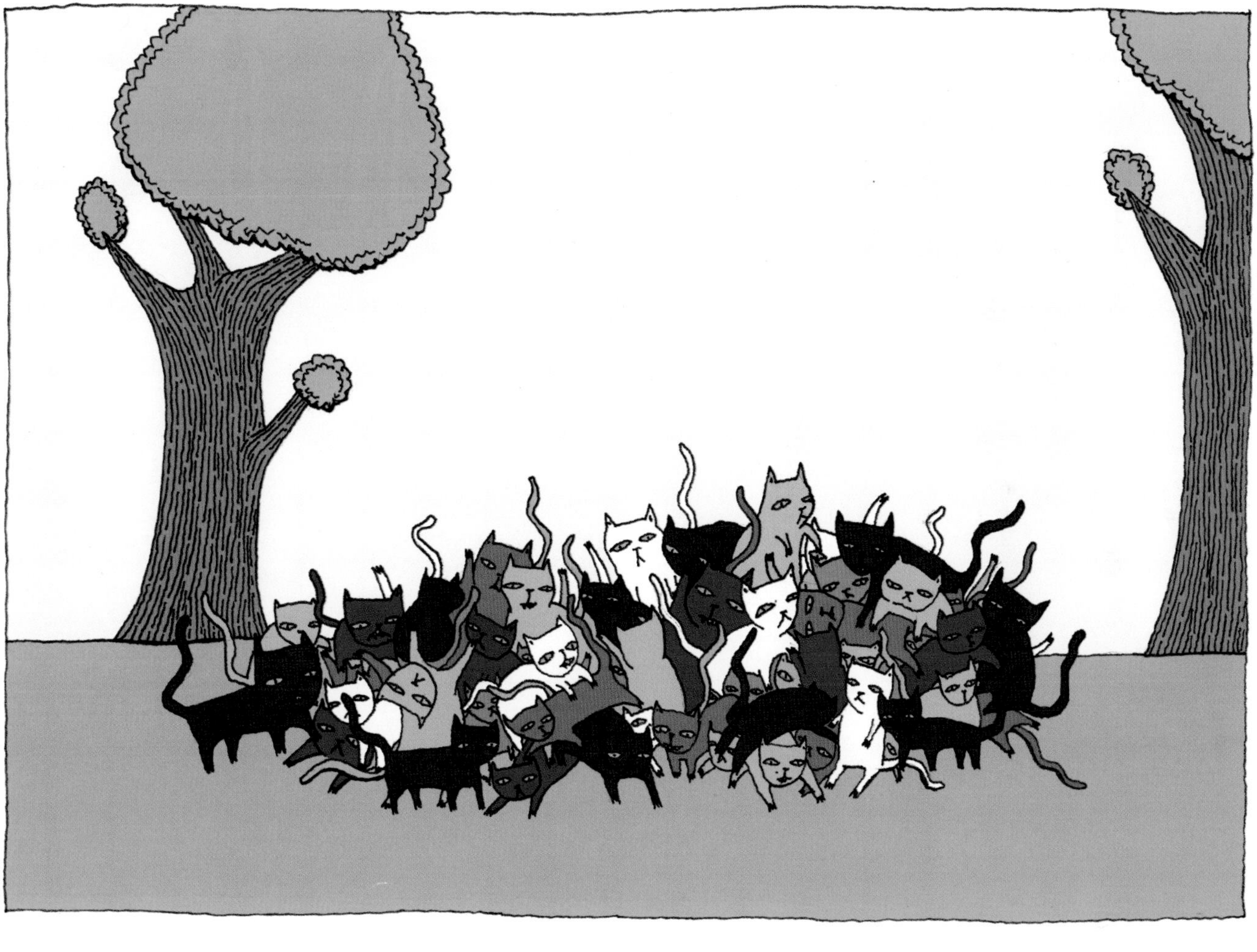

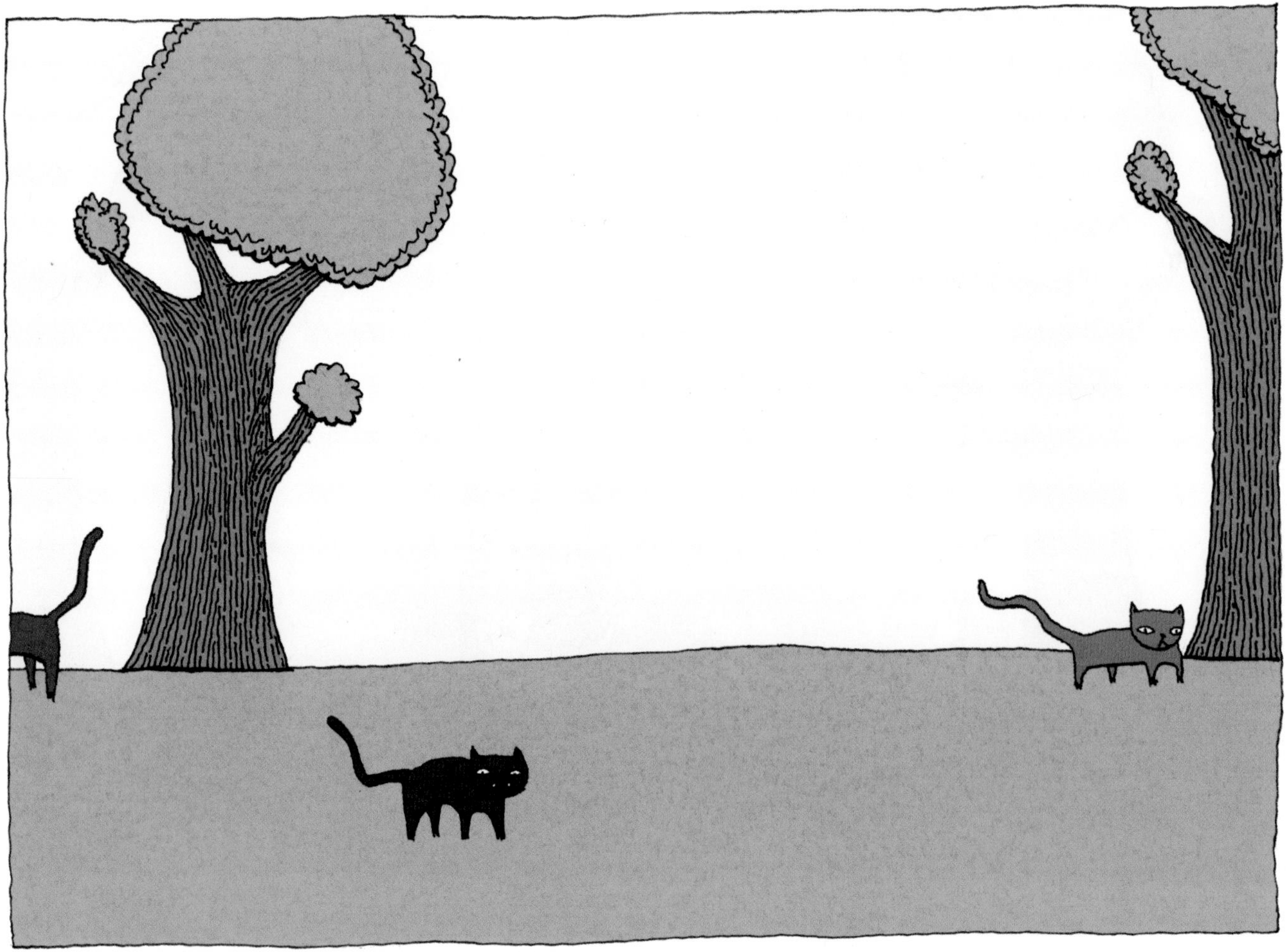

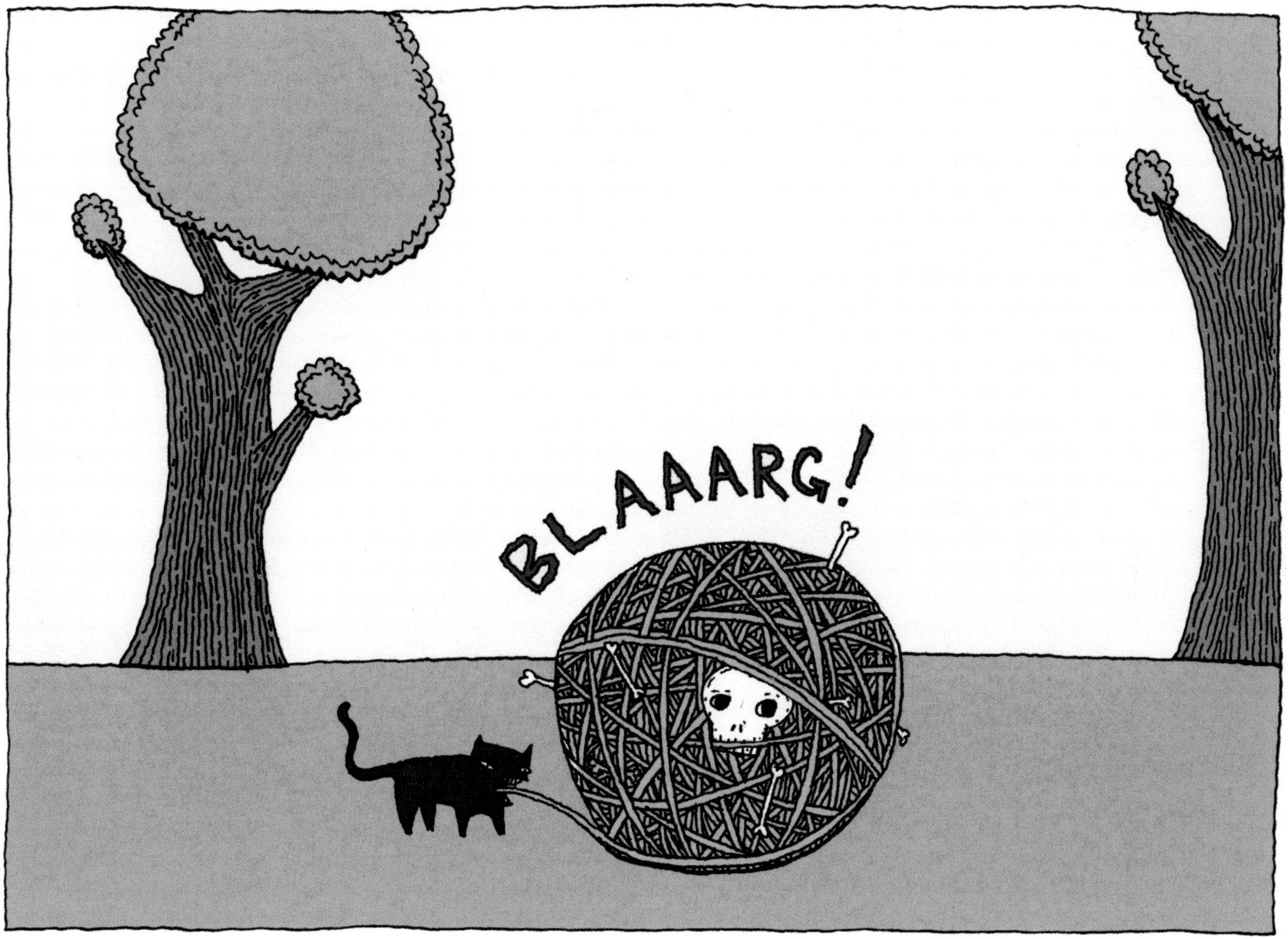
BLAARG!

Pinocchio's Dentist

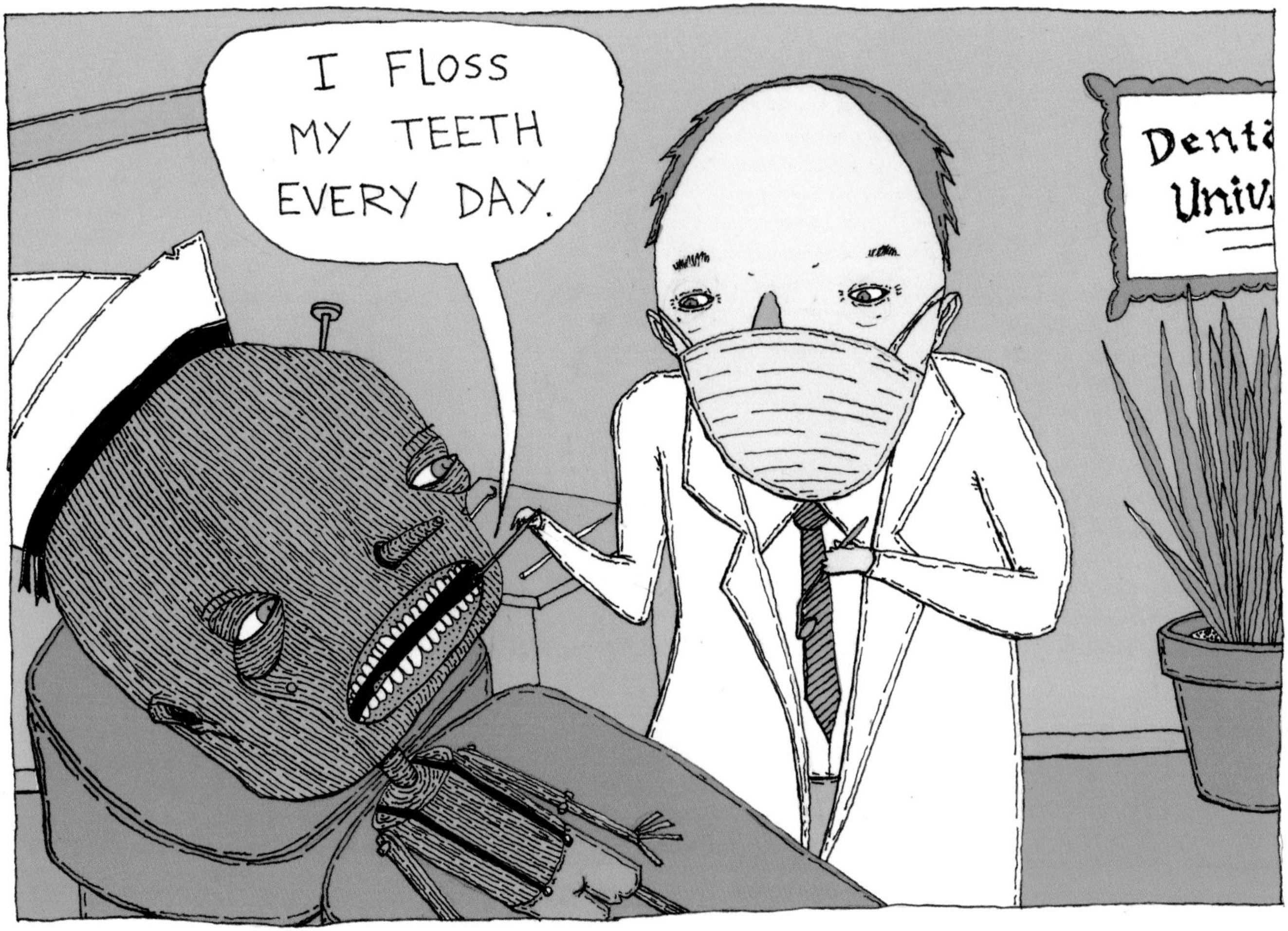
I FLOSS MY TEETH EVERY DAY.
Dent
Univ

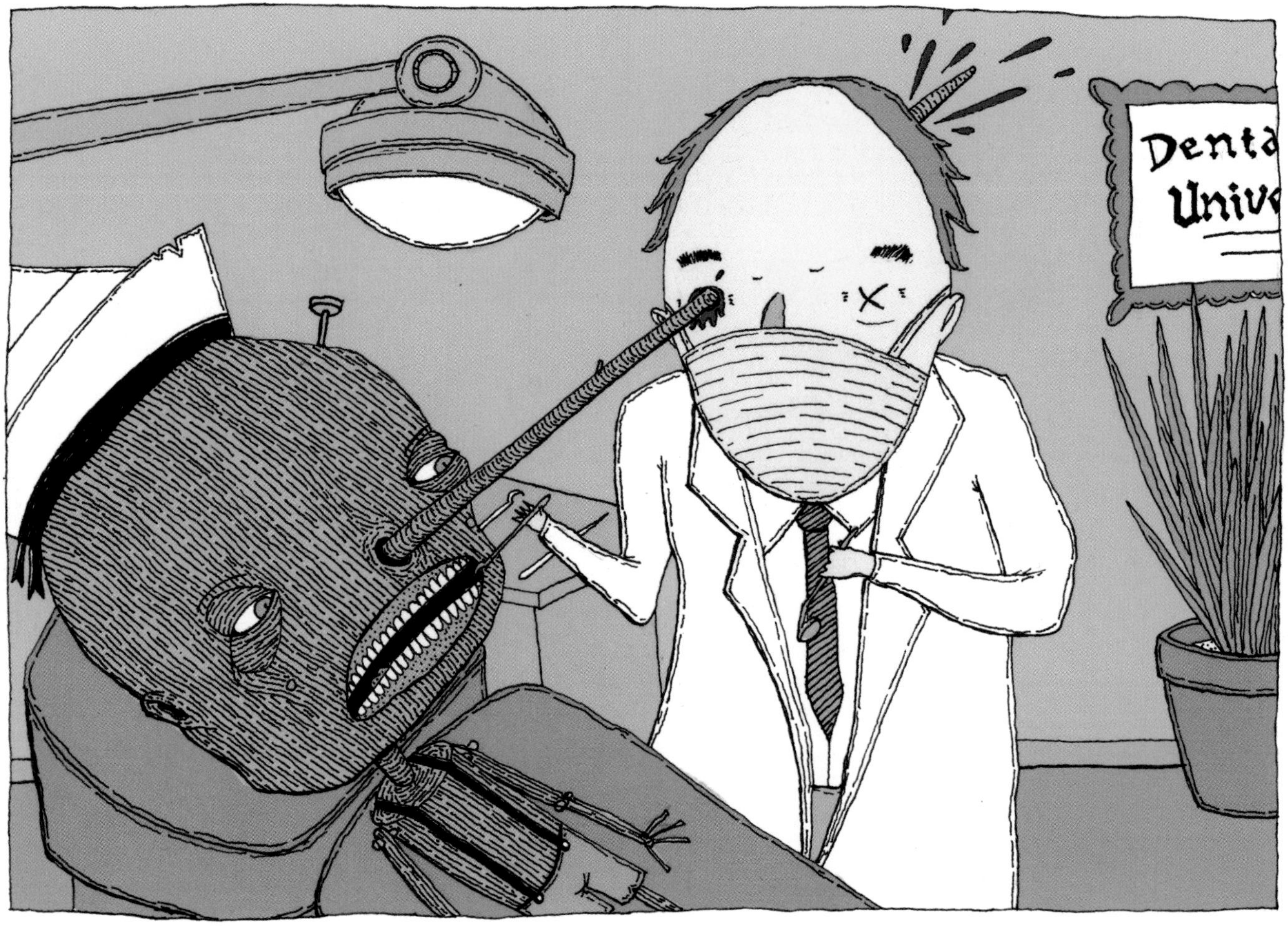
Denta
Unive

Humpty Gets Laid

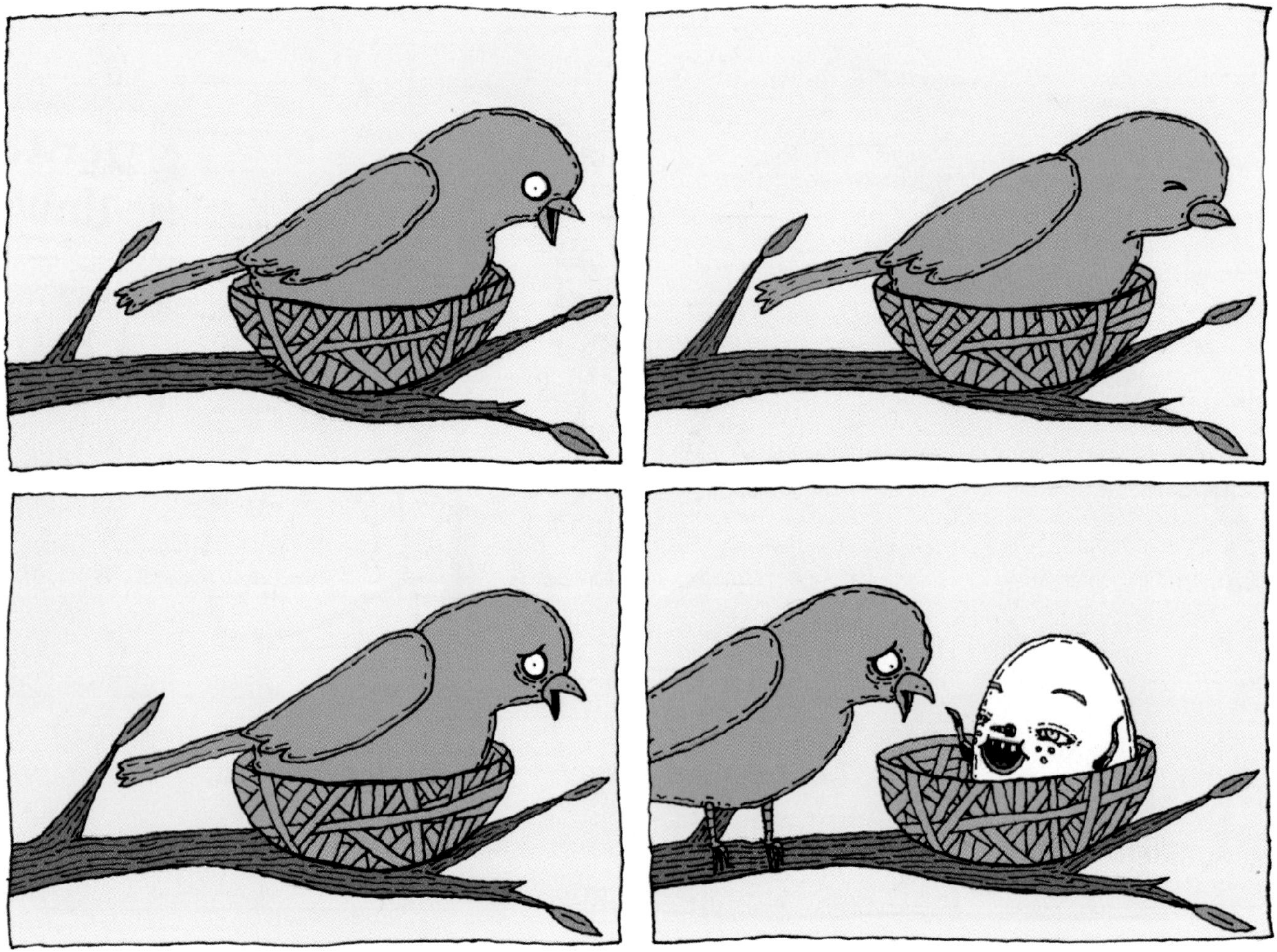

Great Aquatic Romance #3

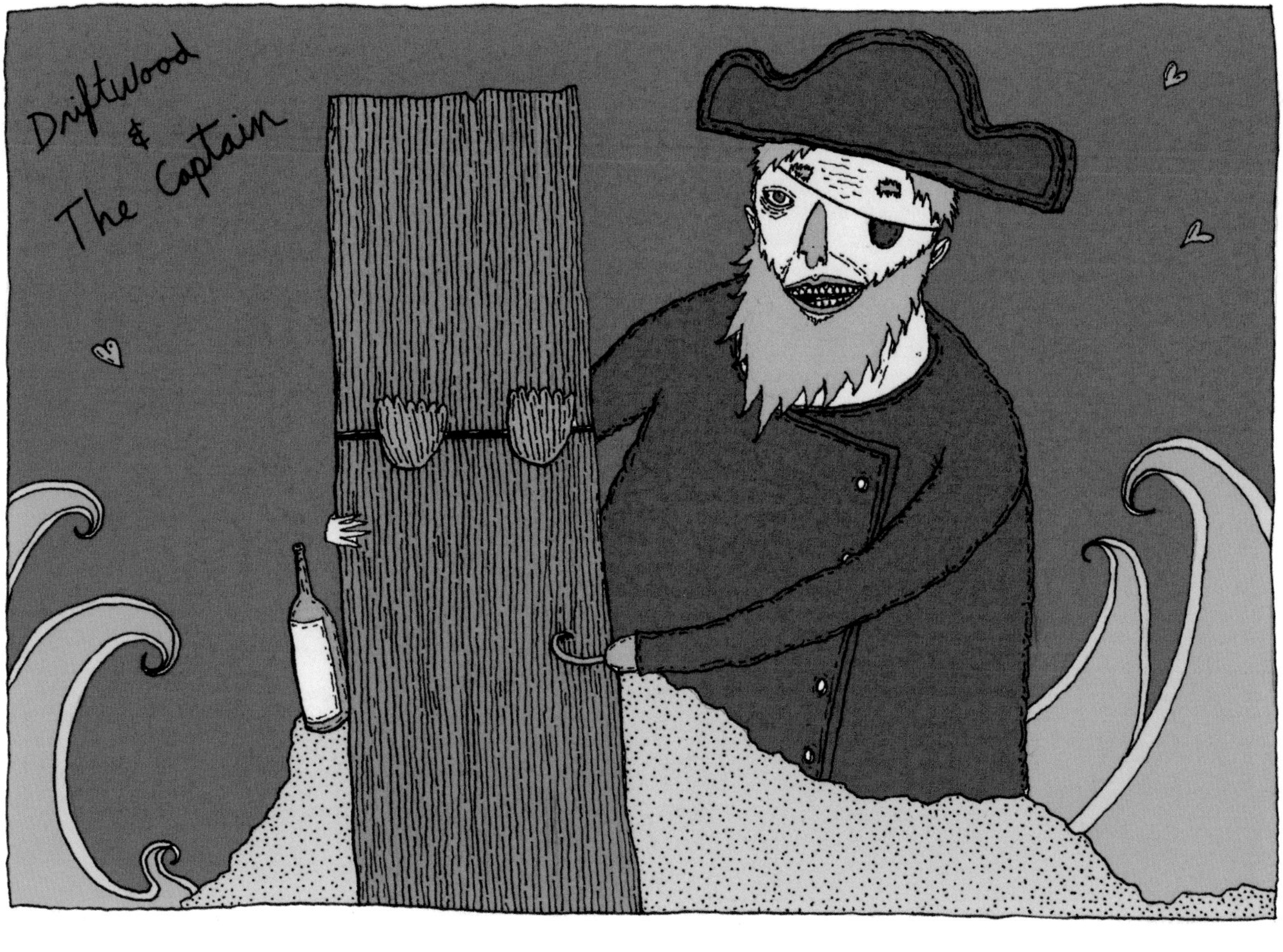
Driftwood
&
The Captain

Pattes de Grenouilles

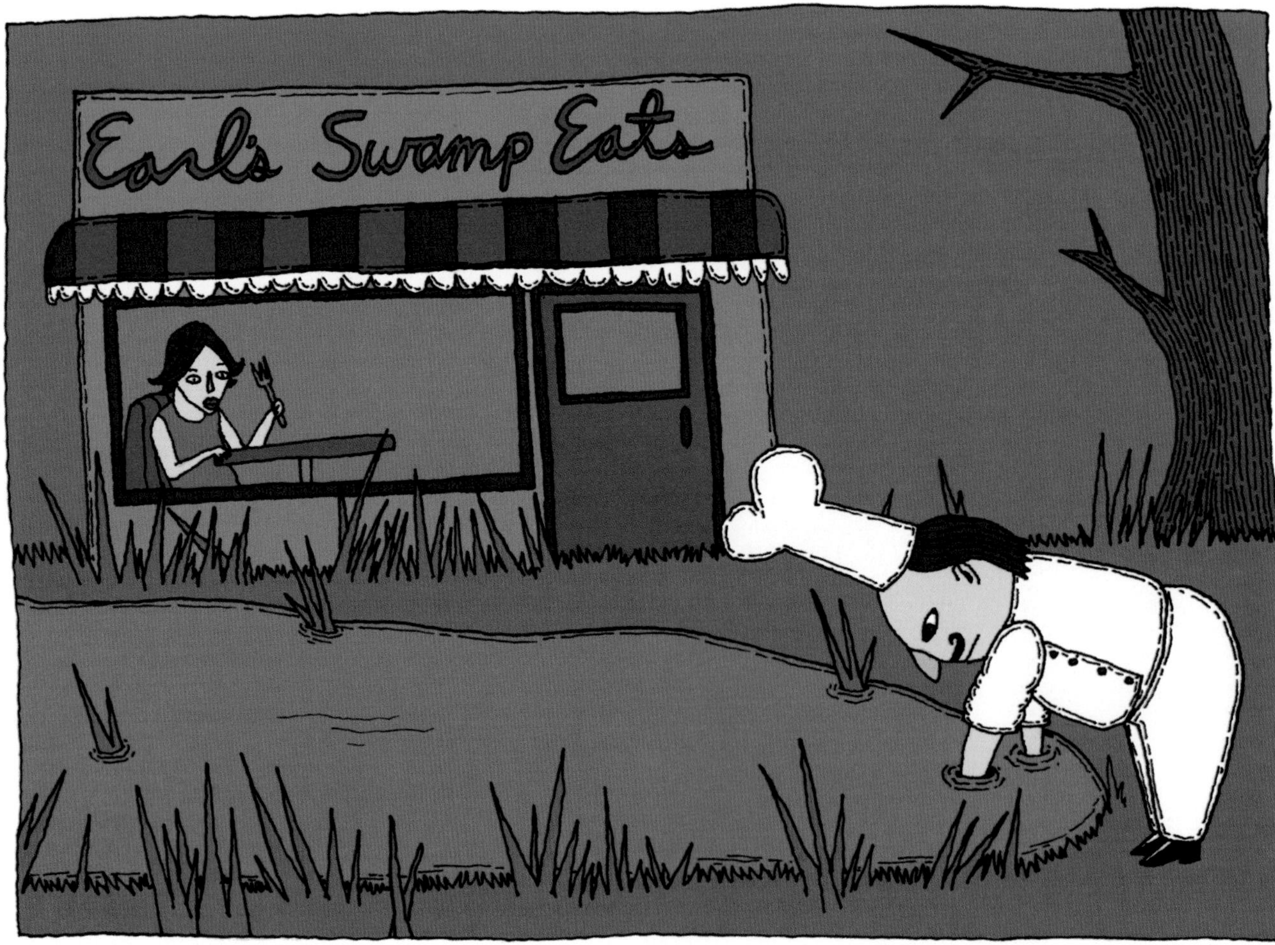
Earl's Swamp Eats

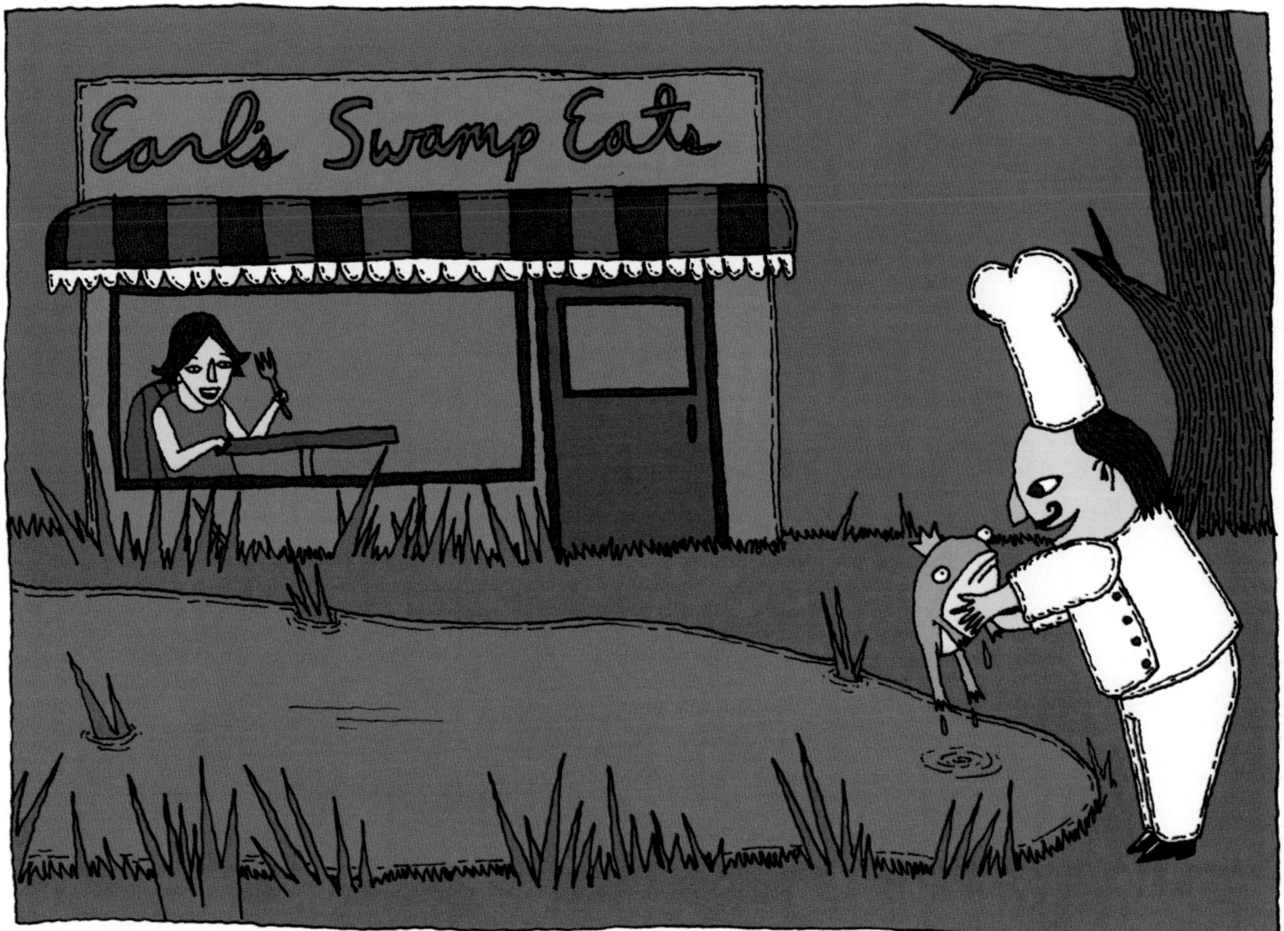
Earl's Swamp Eats

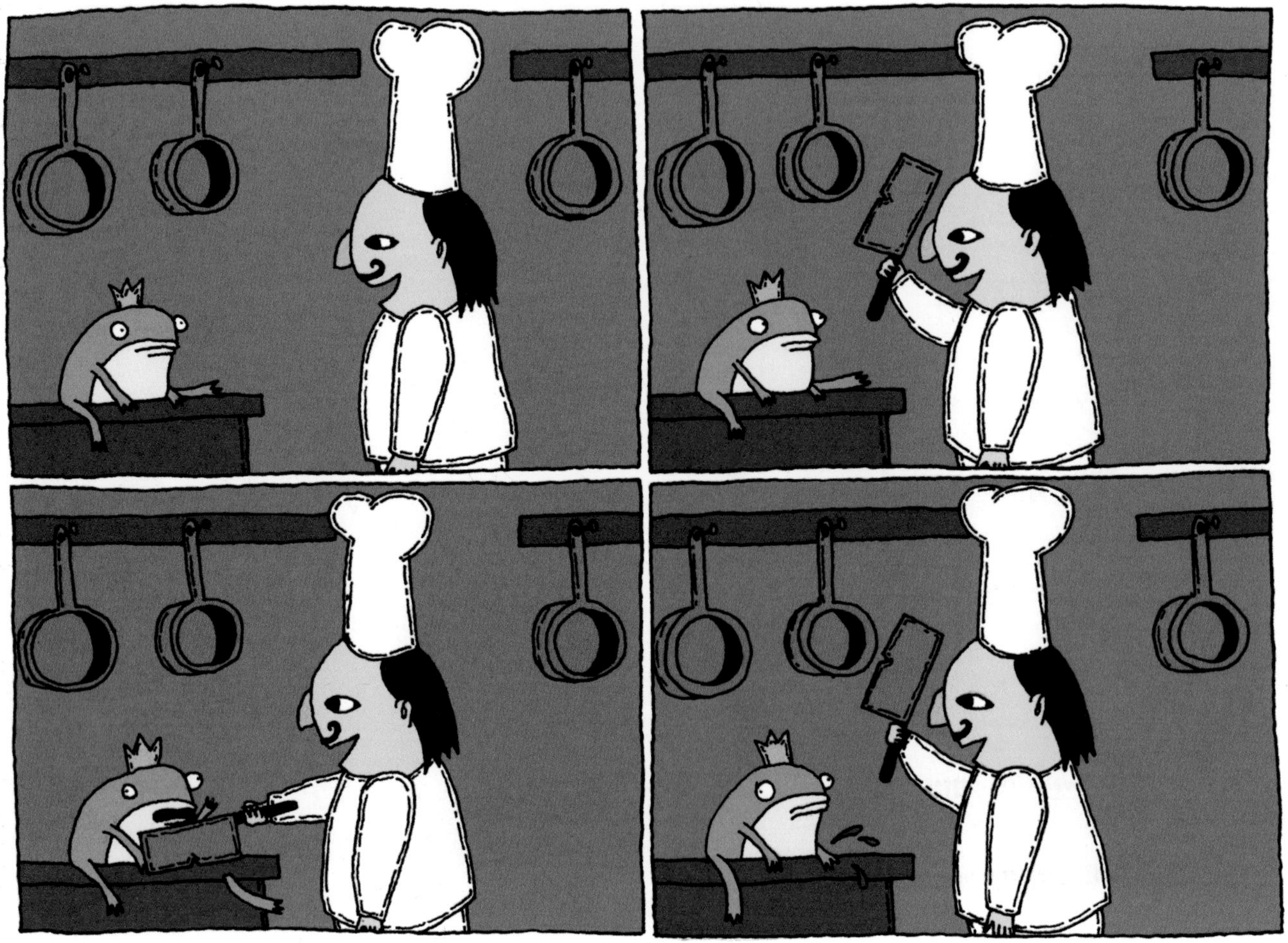

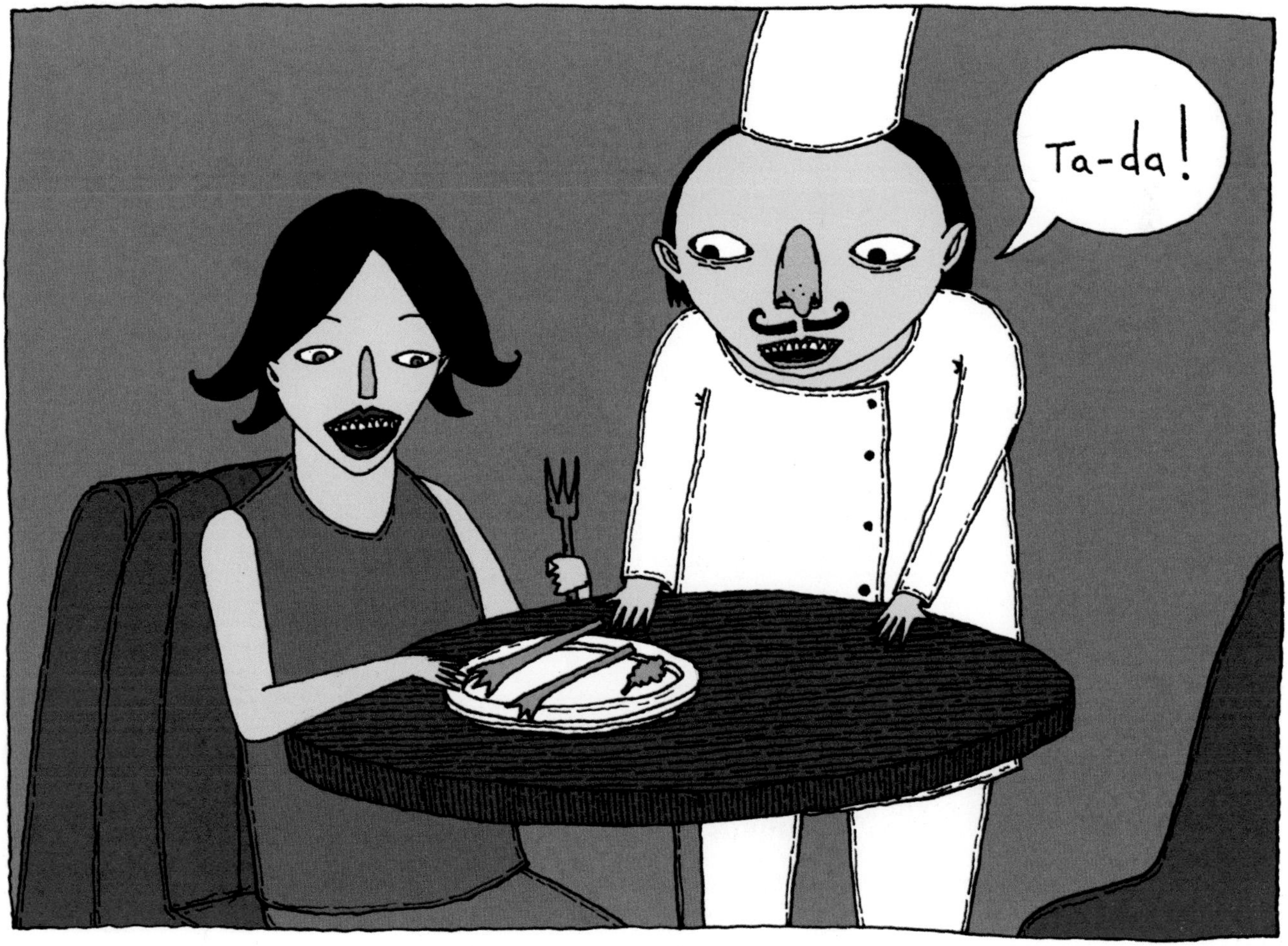
Ta-da!

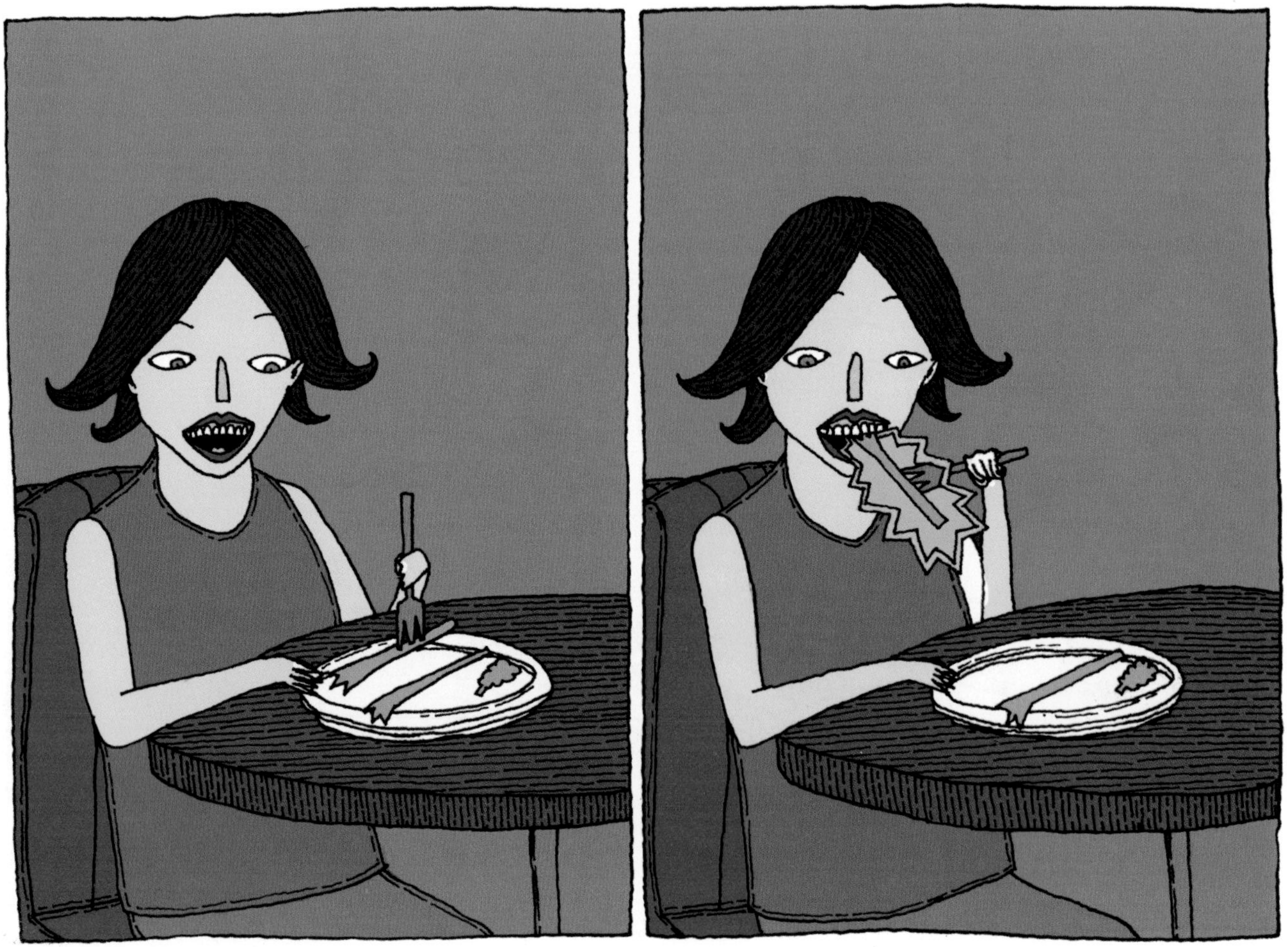

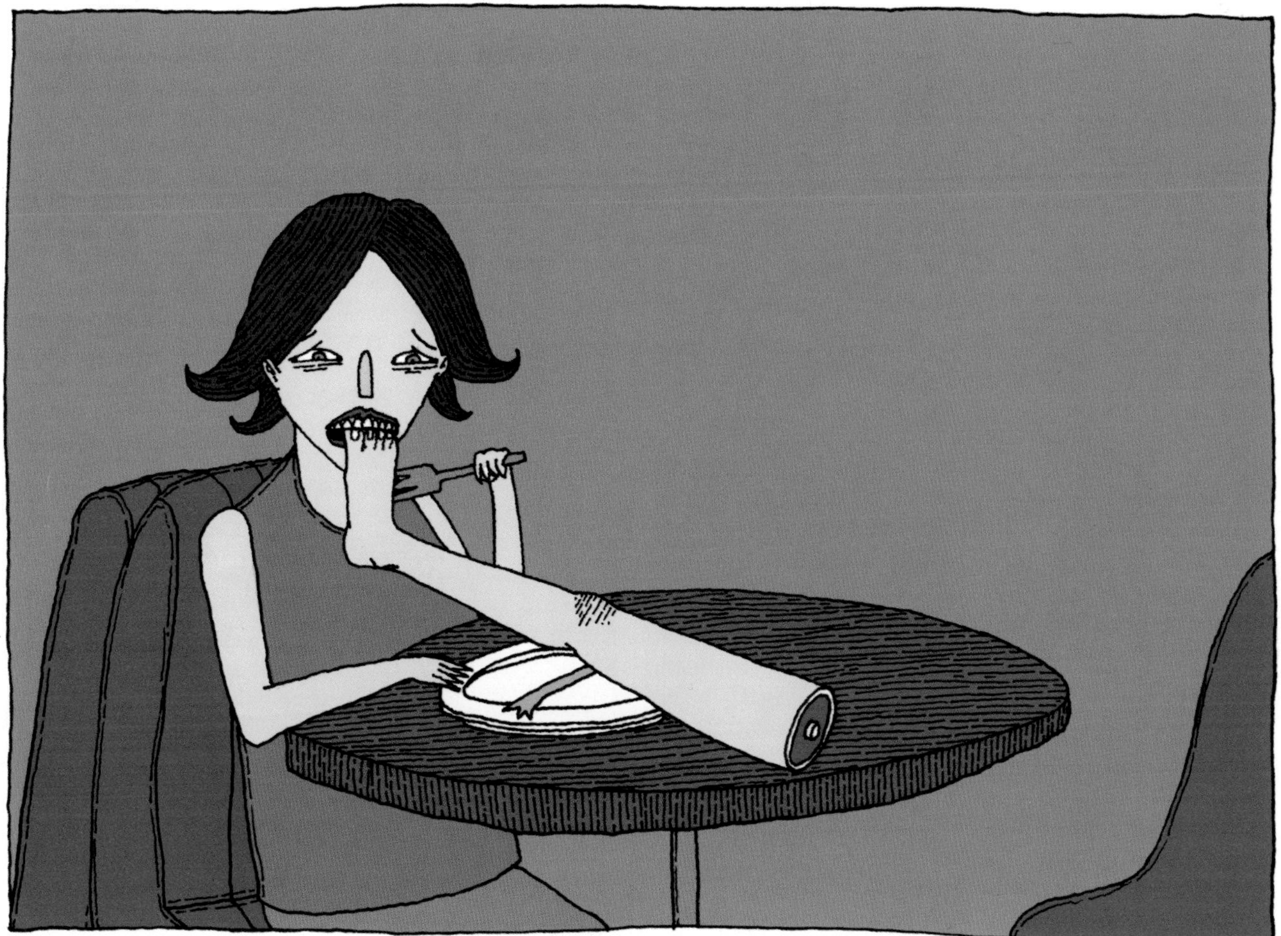

Magic Moments

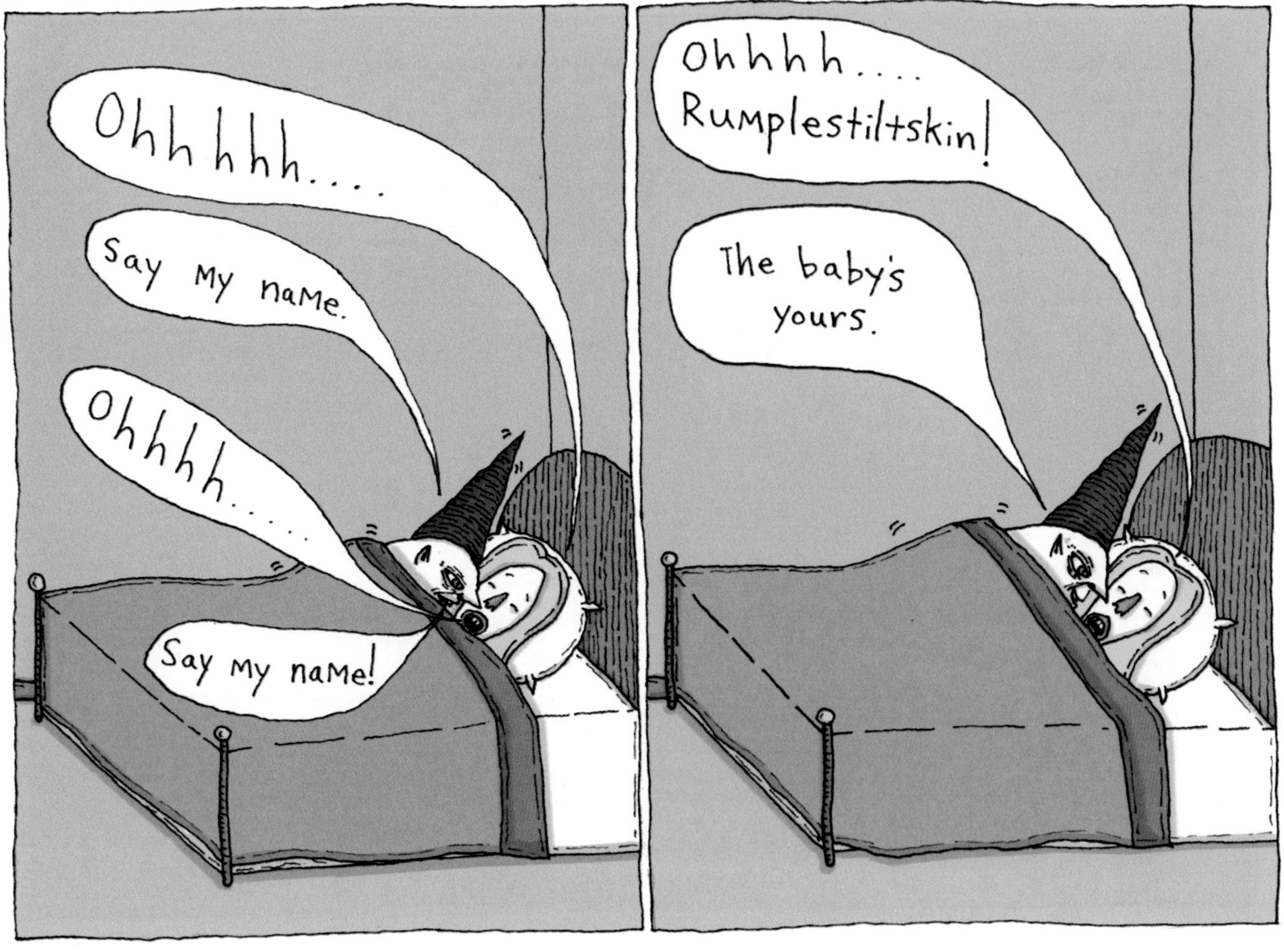
Ohhhhh....
Say my name.
Ohhhh.....
Say my name!
Ohhhh....
Rumplestiltskin!
The baby's yours.

Cinderella's Dress

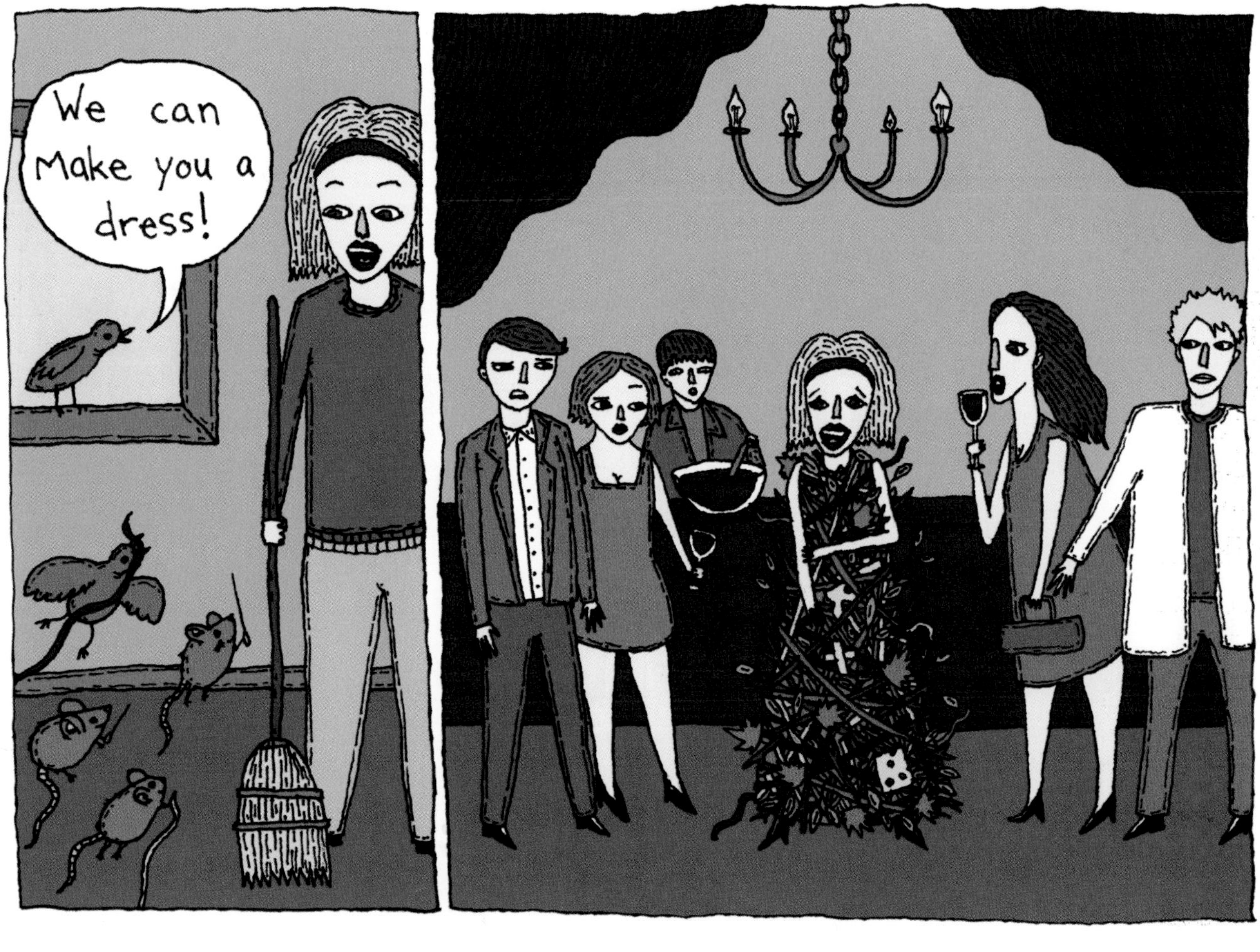
We can Make you a dress!

Rip Van Drinkle

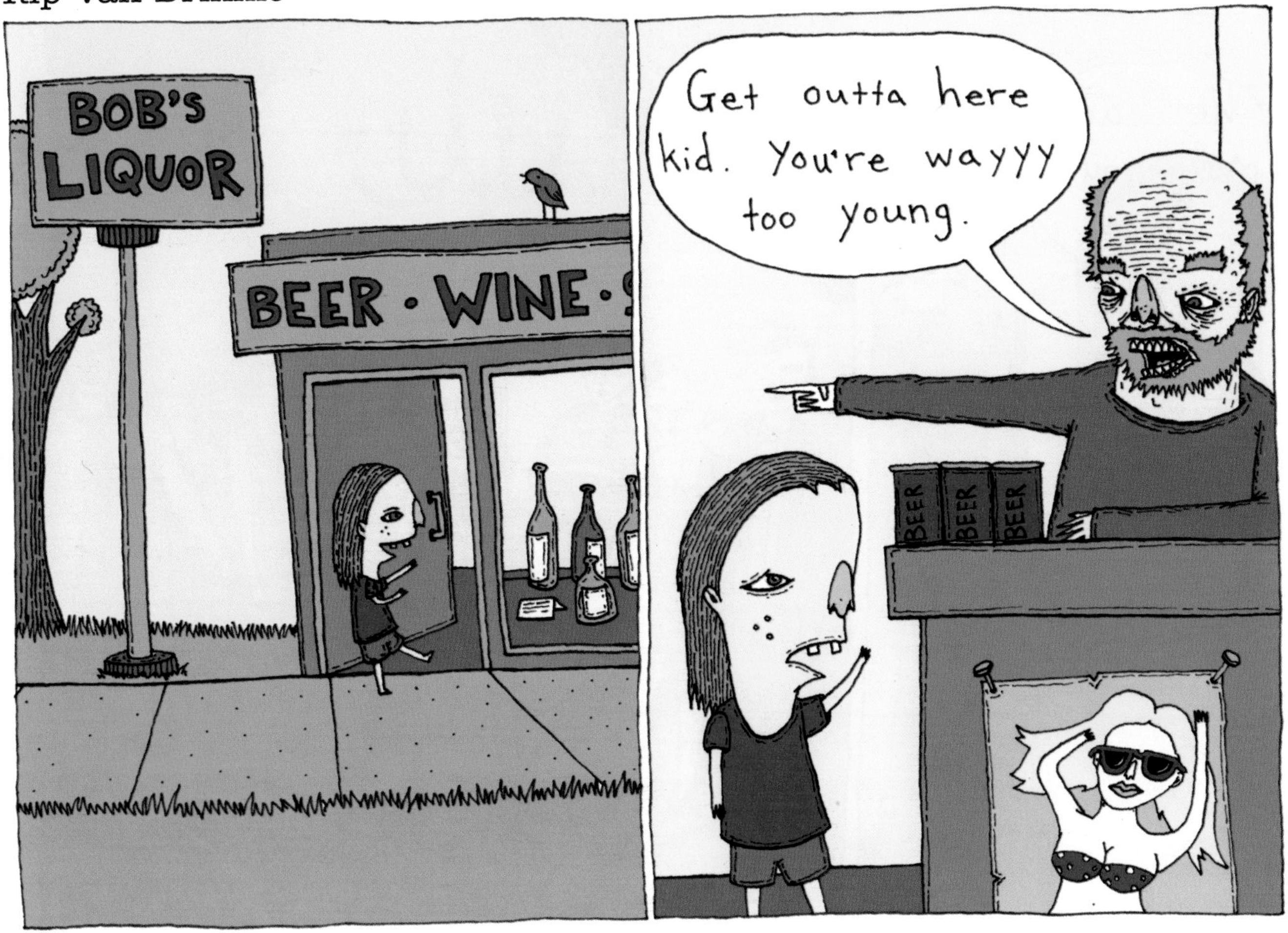
BOB'S LIQUOR
BEER · WINE ·
Get outta here kid. You're wayyy too young.
BEER
BEER
BEER

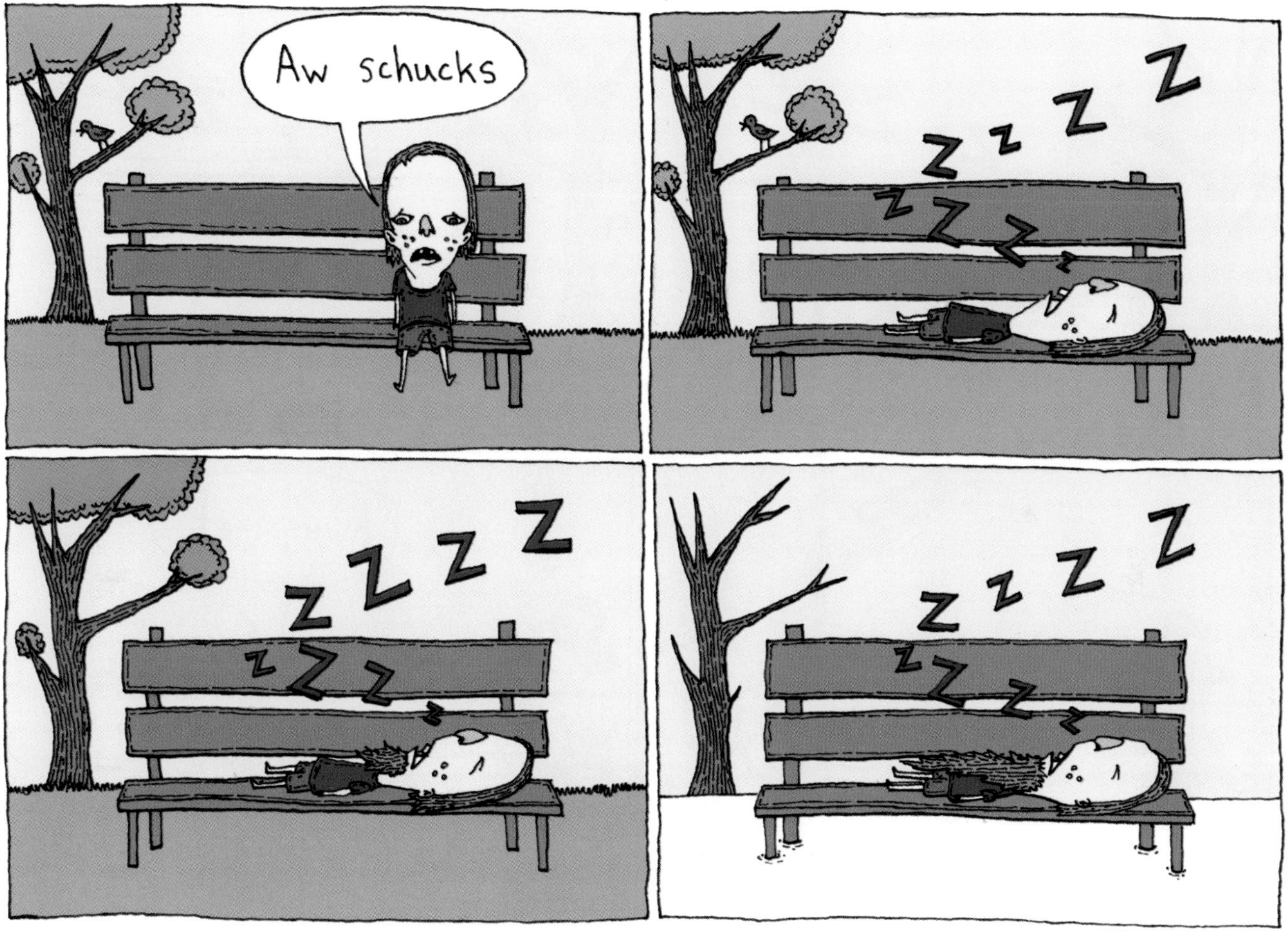
Aw schucks

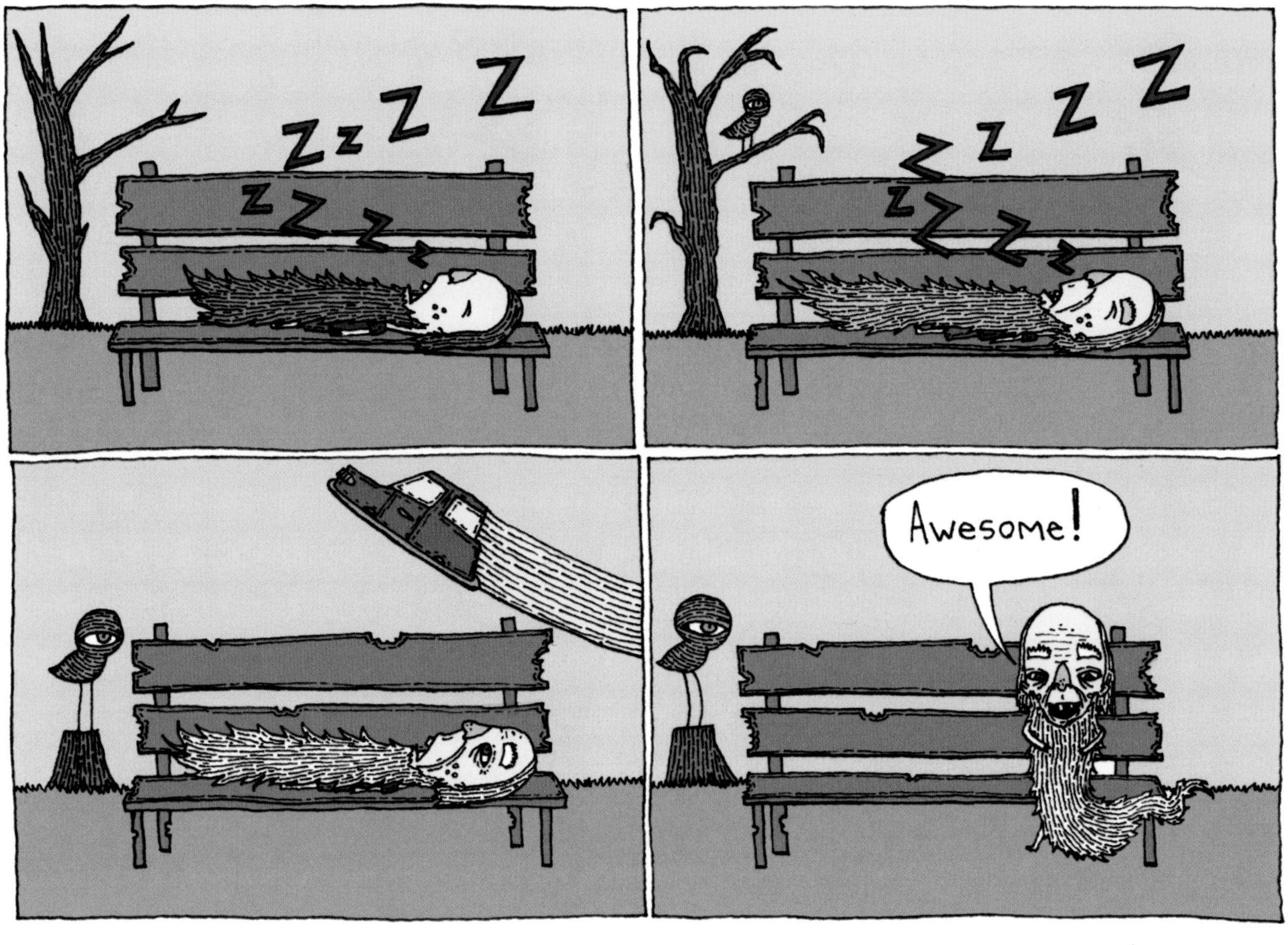
Z z Z Z
z Z Z z
Z Z Z Z
Z Z Z z
Awesome!

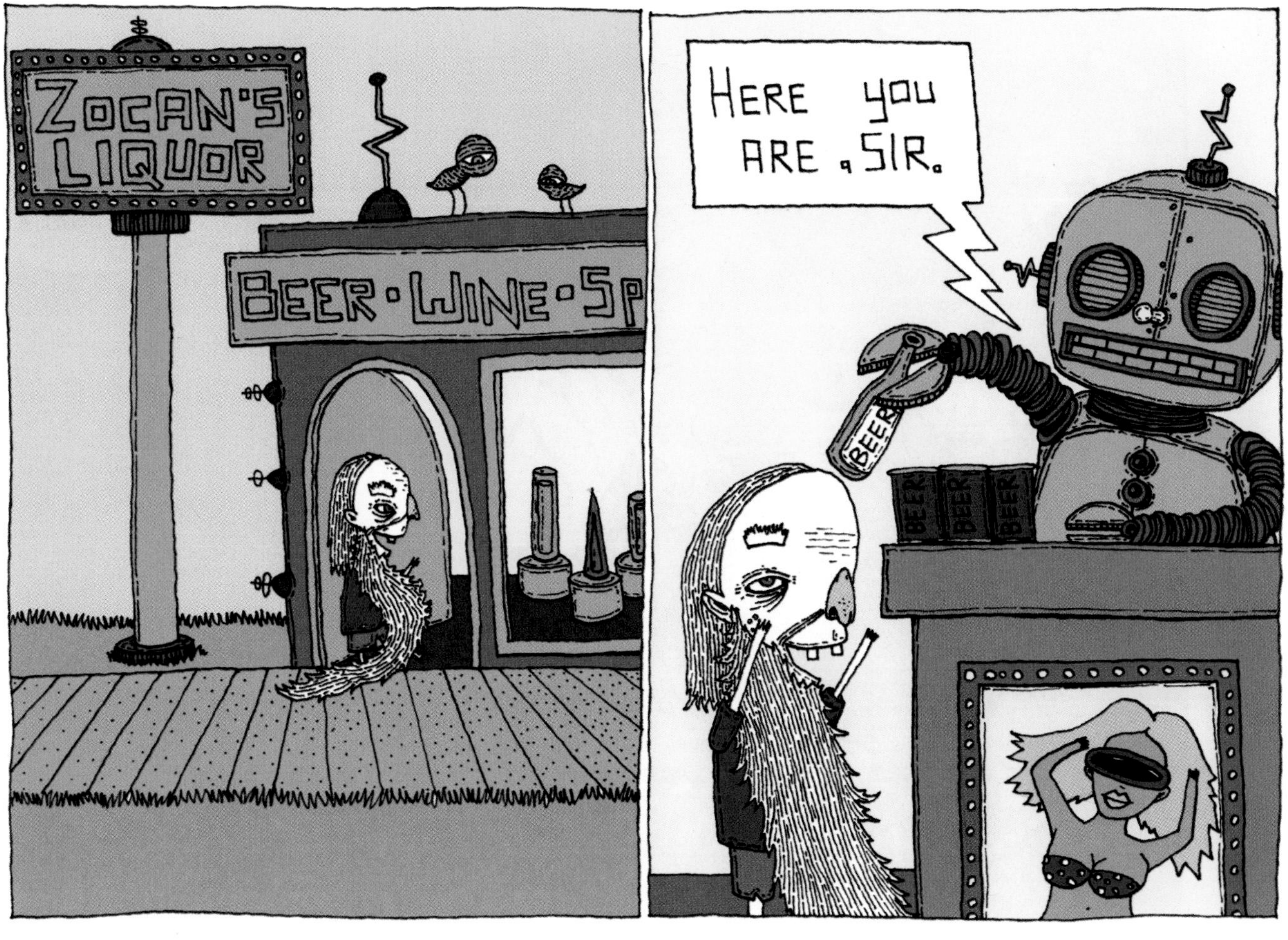
ZOCAN'S LIQUOR
BEER • WINE • SP
HERE you ARE, SIR.
BEER
BEER
BEER
BEER

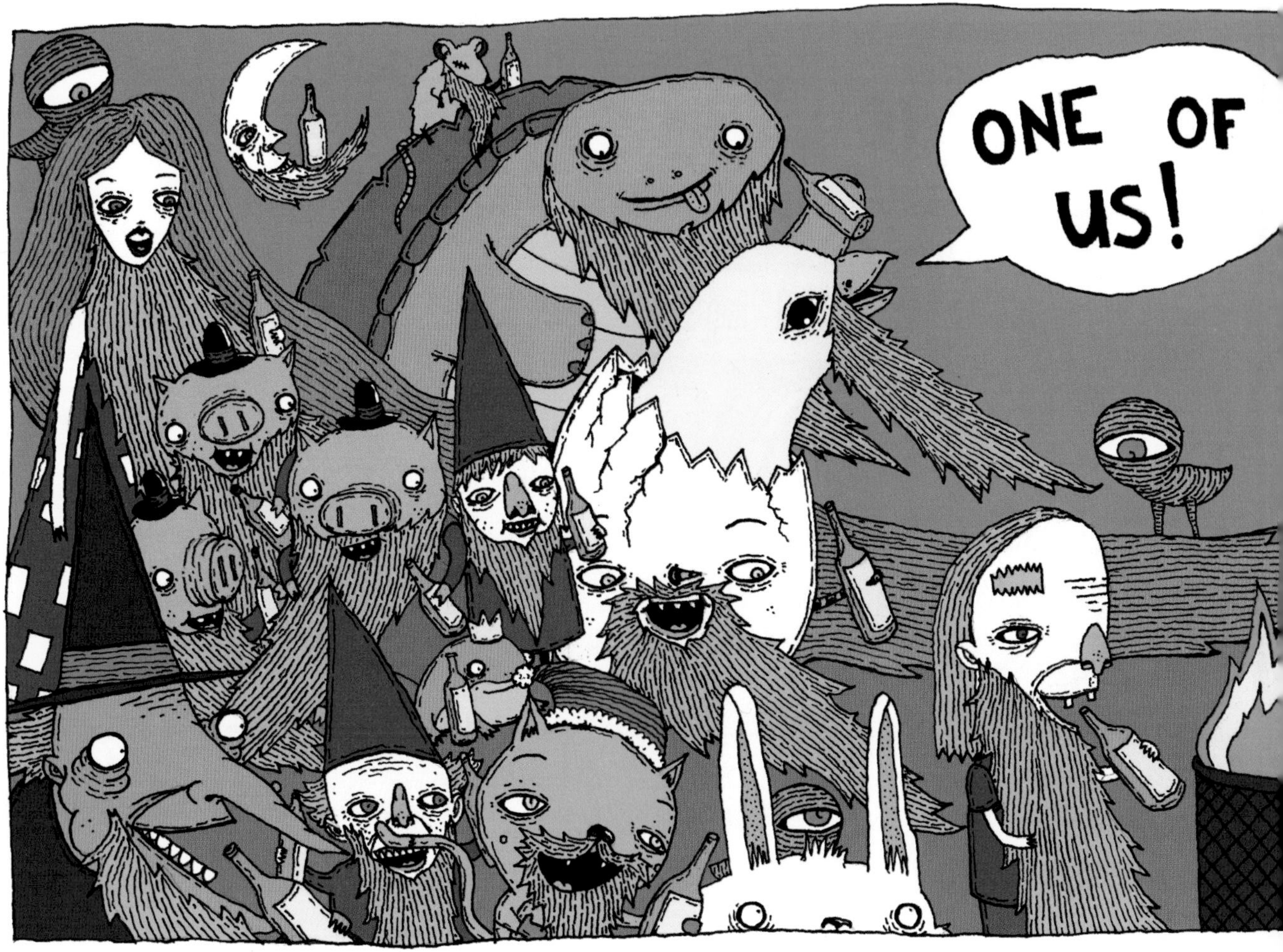
ONE OF US!

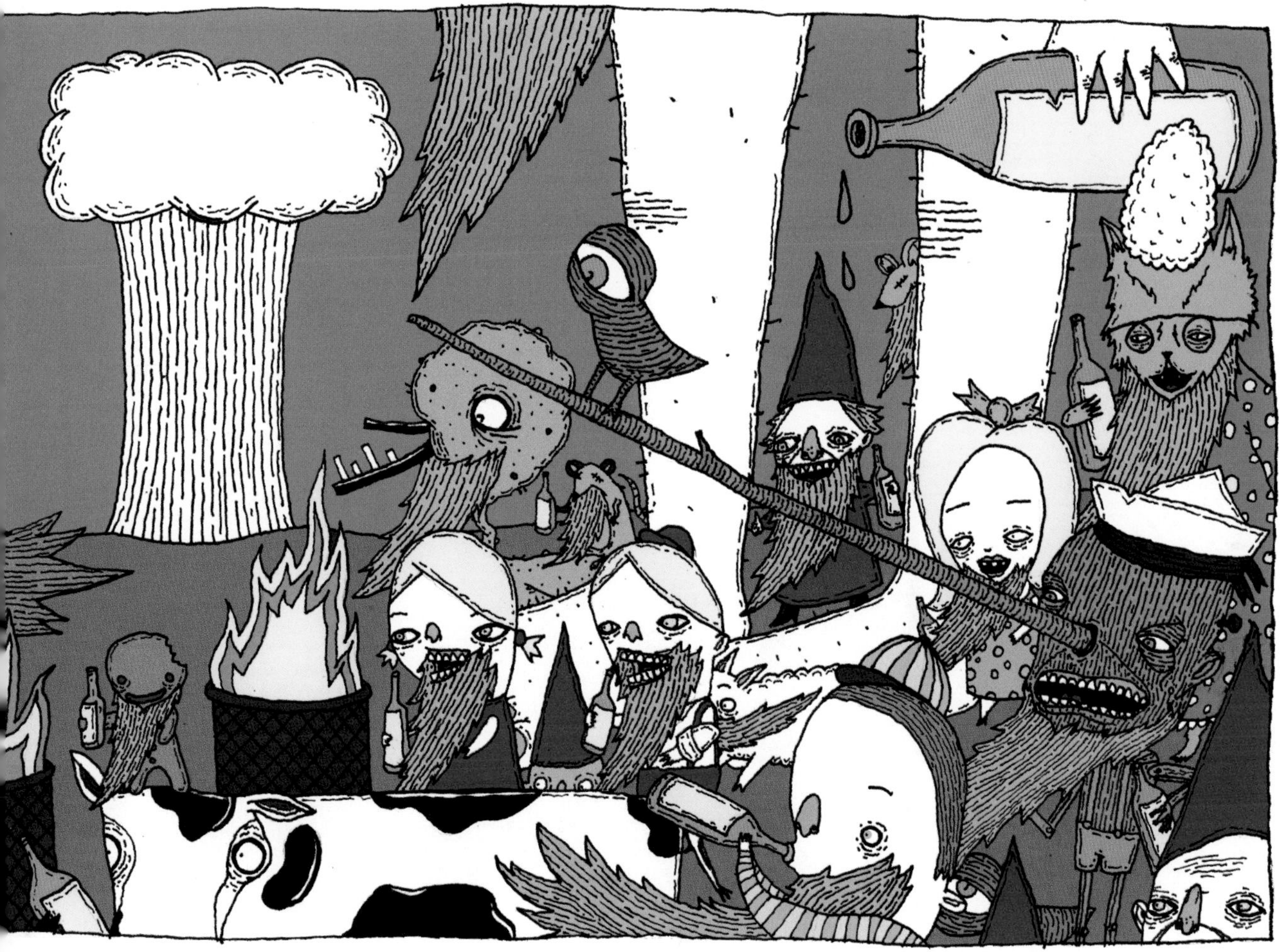